A MARRIAGE MANUAL
FOR FORMER
HOMOSEXUALS

Kent A. Philpott, MDiv, DMin

EVM

Earthen Vessel Media, LLC

MARRIAGE MANUAL FOR FORMER HOMOSEXUALS
©2021 by Kent Philpott

First created in 1980 as a doctoral thesis by the author at San Francisco
Theological Seminary in San Anselmo, California.

Earthen Vessel Media, LLC
San Rafael, CA 94903
www.earthenvesselmedia.com

ISBN: 978-1-946794-31-4 print
        978-1-946794-32-1 eBook

Library of Congress Control Number: 2021949302

Transcribed by Stephanie Adams
Cover design by Mary Keydash
Interior design by KLC Philpott

All Biblical Scripture quotations, unless otherwise indicated, are
taken from the Holy Bible, Revised Standard Version® (RSV®),
1952 by the National Council of the Churches of Christ.

Contents

Preface

Now after fifty-two years of the writing of the Marriage Manual for Former Homosexuals as a thesis for a DMin degree at San Francisco Theological Seminary (Presbyterian, USA), in San Anselmo, California, it has come time for its publication.

In recent years, we have again been writing about homosexual and transgender issues. We published two books via our publishing house, Earthen Vessel Media, LLC. The first was in 2020, entitled The Third Sex? Revisited: Homosexual and Transgender Issues from a Biblical Perspective and then in 2021, In the Wrong Body: Transgender Issues from a Biblical Perspective.

In addition, we have interviewed ex-gay and ex-transgender persons for our television program, Why We Are Christians. These programs can be found by going to earthenvesselmedia.com or via the "Miller Avenue Church" free app on many platforms.

Because of responses to those who have read these books and communicated with us, we decided it was time to publish this marriage manual. It contains adult-only material.

We do not do "conversion therapy," and neither did Love In Action. In the 1970s, when few were proud to be gay, there were those who wanted out of that life. Despite the pride movement, there are still those who want out of the gay lifestyle, even some of those who marched in gay parades in San Francisco. For many the gay life is not very gay at all.

Many wonder if they can find fulfillment in a biblically orthodox marriage. To be realistic, we must say some may and some may not. There will be those who can have a healthy and loving relationship yet without sexual expressions. There will be those who can have a healthy and loving relationship, including sexual satisfaction.

Yes, some who leave the gay life will still be attracted to those of the same sex, even when heterosexually married. Here is where the desire to live a faithful life and honor our Lord Jesus Christ is a bullwork against falling into sin again. Yes, it is possible to resist even strong temptations to go back to the old ways. As we grow up into Christ, we put on the full armor of God found listed in Ephesians 6:10–18:

> [10] Finally, be strong in the Lord and in the strength of his might. [11] Put on the whole armor of God, that you may be able to stand against the schemes of the devil. [12] For we do not wrestle against flesh and blood, but against the rulers, against the authorities, against the cosmic powers over this present darkness, against the spiritual forces of evil in the heavenly places. [13] Therefore take up the whole armor of God, that you may be able to withstand in the evil day, and having done all, to stand firm. [14] Stand therefore, having fastened on the belt of truth, and having put on the breastplate of righteousness, [15] and, as shoes for your feet, having put on the readiness given by the gospel of peace. [16] In all circumstances take up the shield of faith, with which you can extinguish all the flaming darts of the evil one; [17] and take the helmet of salvation, and the sword of the Spirit, which is the word of God, [18] praying at all times in the Spirit, with all prayer and supplication. To that end, keep alert with all perseverance, making supplication for all the saints, ...

Few know the battle, the wrestling against powerful bodily forces plus the schemes of the devil, like those who seek to honor their Lord Jesus and turn from sexual sin. Indeed, there are stories of people who have fallen away and have gotten mired once again in homosexuality. Yet, there are the stories of many who turned their eyes upon Jesus and by the power of the Holy Spirit have resisted the wiles of their enemy, Satan.

May this be so for those who examine this volume.

NOTE: Some material is this current volume has been updated to reflect currect societal and historical conditions.

Introductions

ORIGINAL INTRODUCTION

This is written for persons coming out of homosexuality and who may consider heterosexual marriage.

"Once gay, always gay" is a well-known slogan in the homosexual community. Uncritical acceptance of such a statement has led some people to believe they are terminally gay. However, this highly pessimistic concept is challenged by a growing number of persons who are finding there is the possibility of leaving homosexuality behind. I have observed this through the Christian ministry Love In Action, of which, until 1978, I was a part. This evangelical Christian organization was established in 1973 in San Rafael, California, and worked exclusively with persons from a gay background. Several dozen people turned from a homosexual orientation through Love In Action's work. "Once gay, always gay" is a slogan only and not a truth.

The centuries-old gospel message of "repent and believe" has the power to change lives. God's grace in Jesus Christ reaches to all who allow themselves to listen and respond in faith. Persons who believed themselves trapped in a homosexual lifestyle have found new directions through the biblical message.[1] Others, too, outside of a Christian context, have experienced their sexual orientation change from homo- to heterosexual.[2]

---

1   Kent Philpott, *The Third Sex?* (Plainfield, New Jersey: Logos International, 1975) and *The Gay Theology* (Plainfield, New Jersey: Logos International, 1977).

2   Lawrence J. Hatterer, *Changing Homosexuality in the Male* (New York: McGraw-Hill Book Company, 1970).

Although conducted nearly a generation ago, the Masters and Johnson study of homosexuality, *Homosexuality in Perspective*, surprisingly reported that between 1968 and 1977, sixty-seven homosexuals (fifty-four men and thirteen women) wanted to be heterosexual.[3] Though a precise success rate is not reported, the failure rate is currently 35% and is not expected to exceed 45%. On the basis of such findings, Time concluded: "It would mean that a permanent, or at least long-term, switch to heterosexuality is possible more than half the time among gays who are highly motivated to change."[4] This is likely still the same—there are those who have a desire, hope may be a better term, to leave homosexual behavior behind, and if possible, move toward heterosexuality.

Contrary to popular opinion, and contrary to much that comes from the gay community itself, Christian organizations like Love In Action do not preach a message that includes a demand for a gay person to become heterosexual. The content of repentance is to cease sinful behavior; there may yet be homosexual temptations, fantasies, and thought patterns. However, many persons begin to consider a heterosexual lifestyle and marriage, though they once had no thought of being anything but homosexual. My personal concern for friends from gay backgrounds who are investigating the possibility of heterosexual marriage has prompted the writing of this volume.

It is likely that this manual may have applicability to heterosexuals as well as to homosexuals. Though the material is slanted for specific use for persons from a gay background and problems peculiar to that circumstance, heterosexual people may find this manual serviceable. Biblical principles extend to all people, and many difficulties experienced by homosexuals can be encountered by heterosexuals.

It is my conviction that homosexuals are not born that way. So many other factors may enter in, and there is not space here to adequately address these. However desperately a person may want to believe they were born gay, on the basis of what is clear in the Bible, both Old and New Testament, homosexuality is not natural. There are complex and complicating factors. For instance, inherited body types

---

3   William H. Masters and Virginia Johnson, *Homosexuality in Perspective* (Boston: Little, Brown and Co., 1979).
4   *Time*, "Masters and Johnson on Homosexuality," April 23, 1979, p. 78.

may elicit different responses from peers. A boy who was born with a slight body build may be called a "sissy," thus possibly producing a crisis of identity. A girl who carries genes that result in a boyish figure may well find that unconsciously she is steered toward a gay identity. There are the parenting issues, a mother wanting a girl but has a boy, or the reverse. Or, the influence may come from a father who wanted a boy but has a girl. And then there are the hormonal factors, brain chemistry issues, and many other mysterious and complex influences. Still, despite all the complications and quirks of nature, no divine or malevolent hand intervened to confuse sexuality.

Homosexual identity is not necessarily then a choice; rarely does a person decide to be homosexual. Again, influences, primarily parental in the early years, largely determine sexual identity. If patterns are learned, then they can be unlearned and new patterns established. And the interior working of The Spirit of God, can facilitate and encourage relearning and provide changing power through the ministry of love, forgiveness, and regeneration. It is a cooperative venture between God and human beings, much in line with Paul's statement, "For this I toil, struggling with all his energy that he powerfully works within me."[5]

Theologically, I am conservative in my approach to Scripture as understood in the contemporary Christian community. Those attracted to this marriage manual will largely be from this community and are persons who do not want to live their lives as a gay person. These folk may be wondering if living in a heterosexual marriage relationship is possible for them. For those who do not feel they can ever be fully heterosexual and see no hope for marriage themselves, this manual may provide useful material for friends.

---

5   Colossians 1:29. Also see 1 Corinthians 15:10, Philippians 2:13 and 4:13, and Ephesians 3:20. All Biblical references will be from the *Revised Standard Version* of the Bible, unless otherwise indicated.

INTRODUCTION TO THE CURRENT VOLUME

In 1978, I left the ministry of Love In Action at the request of Frank Worthen and those who were, at that point, leading that outreach to gay people. Ever since, I have had a heart for people with same-sex attraction, especially for those who recognize homosexual behavior or activity as sinful.

Are some of us human beings born with same-sex attraction? That question may be unanswerable, but I have known many who sincerely believed this was true for them. Yet, upon taking a close look at the nature of parent-child relationships, we often glimpsed some factors that might have contributed to an attraction for the same sex. Even so, for a rather high percentage of people whom I counseled and ministered to over the years, we found that even after years of being followers of Jesus, the homosexual attraction was still their reality. These dear folk, though sometimes "slipping" and experiencing severe attacks of guilt and shame, would continue being devoted to their Lord Jesus Christ who they knew loved them and had taken all their sins upon Himself.

There are some who identify with the church of which I am senior pastor whom I suspect experience same-sex attraction. They are mostly silent about their orientation yet have been able to remain celibate despite everything. Actually, I would love it if one or more of them, male or female, who are same-sex attracted, would step up and engage in outreach to people like themselves in our little Miller Avenue Baptist Church, or who are hoping to be part of a church who knows and understands them.

I continue to receive phone calls, mostly early Sunday mornings, when a voice asks, "I am gay. Can I come to your church?" I always say, "Yes." But they never come. Perhaps it is fear that prevents them from attending and identifying themselves to me, or maybe it is just a spoof, or something else I do not understand.

Our hope is that this current volume, presented now so many years after the original marriage manual was first written and whose content comes almost entirely from those who were part of the Love In Action ministry centered in San Rafael, California, during the 1970s, would be of some value to those who struggle with same-sex attraction in our current day and have a hope that perhaps they might find a measure of opposite-sex attraction. However, for those who find that nothing is going to change their same-sex attraction, even as devoted followers of Jesus, I want them to know this is entirely understandable and not a matter of sin.

1
Marriage in Perspective

Marriage is not the prime goal of life. Turning that into a positive statement, it may be said that the chief purpose of our living is to know and love the God who created human beings and gave them the capacity for love. Paul said that we *"have been destined and appointed to live for the praise of his glory" (Ephesians 1:12)*. Marriage is a part, though an important one, of life for the human population on this planet. It is not ultimate, nor is it a requirement for happiness or fulfillment. For marriage to be a healthy and beautiful part of a person's life, whether that person be heterosexual or former homosexual, the relationship of a man and woman in family must be held in proper perspective. Marriage can be either up-building or destructive. When marriage is exaggerated as the great answer to life, it will seem to fail and could become a tragedy rather than a blessing. A former homosexual should look long and hard at marriage before committing himself/herself to it.

A HOMOSEXUAL LOOKS AT MARRIAGE

Fear is the emotion most often mentioned by a homosexual when he/she thinks of marriage. Misogamy, the fear of the opposite sex or the dread of marriage, is common among homosexuals, both practicing and former homosexuals. The elements of this fear are complex, varied, understandable, and hard to define.

FEARS OF MALE HOMOSEXUALS

Men may fear impotence, the problem of performing sexually. After sex with men only a transition to sex with a woman may seem daunting; in fact, such should be expected. The male species must have an erection of the penis before the basic sex act, intercourse, can be accomplished. Normal heterosexuals experience this problem of failing to achieve an erection, too. For the person with a gay past, this fear can be a monster. The thought of such a failure in the presence of an expectant female can be frightfully embarrassing to any man. Of course, various levels of sexuality may be enjoyed without intercourse taking place.

A man may fear the loss of freedom that marriage would bring. Many gay men had mothers who excessively controlled them and could have consequently developed a neurotic love-hate relationship with the mother. This may generalize to include most other women. Marriage for such a person may seem to be a type of bondage, legal and institutionalized. A man does not desire to be married to a tyrant (neither does a woman, for that matter). A male homosexual may tend to see all women as controllers and alternatively love and hate women. Compounding the fear of a loss of freedom would be the prospect of children. Responsibility for "more than me" can be scary. For some, there is also the fear of molesting their own children.

Some male homosexuals have taken the "cathouse test." They have wondered what heterosexuality would be like and have tried it out with a professional or a friend who has consented to a testing. The lackluster and dingy experience of such impersonal sex, especially if it is with a professional, can have a discouraging effect and convince a male gay that homosexuality is far superior to heterosexuality. Unsatisfying and guilt-laden sexual experiments under less than pleasant circumstances may produce fear of additional heterosexual contact.

A man may be apprehensive about the frequency of sex with a woman; fear of too many sexual demands or a fear of not enough sex. The male gay scene is quite sexually oriented. Many who are caught up in the consuming arena of impersonal sexual encounters in gay baths, bars, beaches, park restrooms, and rest stops may experience numerous sexual releases in a 24-hour period. Names may never be exchanged. When a gay person speaks of a lover, he may be referring to an individual whom he has known only a few hours. This is not to say there are no long-term unions between gays, but a new lover every day is not uncommon, especially for younger gay men. The gay scene can be an exhilarating, exciting pursuit of sex in which the anticipation is often more stimulating than the event. It may be characterized by feelings of passion interwoven with the presence of danger, the thrill of experiencing wild heart palpitations as an intended sexual partner is approached. For numerous individuals coming out of a gay background, such conditions have become the norm and closely connected or associated with sex. Without that sense of excitement, sexual arousal may not be reached.

Marriage means then an end to almost every aspect of this type of sexual pursuit. Marriage is long-term, intimate, and personal, and encompasses far more than sexual indulgence. Commitment is called for and support must be extended. Marriage also means responsibility. This can be very frightening for someone who has fled obligations and rebelled against conventional ideas. Ex-gays are often unsure about their capacity to assume accountability for a wife and family. The decision to pledge fidelity to one person, particularly a woman, is not reached easily.

Some men may fear the woman's body, the softness and smoothness of the female body style. Men who have a partiality towards body hair and muscles are going to wonder how they could ever love a smooth body. Psychological stimulation is a key factor in sexual arousal, and for some gay men, a woman's body is not attractive.

Some gay men will fear the female genitals; he has previously sought a penis. The genitals of a woman may appear grotesque and meaningless. This is a matter of psychological response to visual stimuli which is a critical factor in sexual arousal.

Men from a gay background may fear oral sex with a woman. Intercourse may be one thing, but cunnilingus quite another.

There is also the fear of exposure. Some gay men have had hundreds of sexual encounters. It is possible that a former lover may reappear and present himself to a wife or children. Blackmail, harassment, and usually tortuous anguish can result.

The above are simply a cursory and limited discussion of the fears a male homosexual may have to face in contemplating marriage. In light of the fears previously mentioned, marriage could seem an impossible dream for many men from a gay lifestyle.

Frank, open, and honest discussion of delicate issues can make the difference in diffusing fear. Perhaps the one essential ingredient in a marriage between two formerly gay persons or an ex-gay and a heterosexual, is being able to discuss sexual issues freely and openly without guilt and shame. And likely this would take time to develop.

FEARS OF FEMALE HOMOSEXUALS

Women from a homosexual background share many of the fears that trouble a male homosexual. Women fear frigidity, the concern over being able to authentically enjoy sex and provide satisfaction for a mate. A woman can "fake it," but most women will become inpatient with that kind of sex. A woman who has a difficult time being sexually aroused by a man will certainly fear engaging in the sexual act.

A husband is going to mean a loss of freedom and it is difficult to walk out of a legal marriage, especially if children are involved. There can be increased financial and social pressure, and the trauma associated with breaking up a family of three-plus is severe.

Many gay women have engaged in sexual relations with men, usually in their younger years. The conditions of such sexual encounters were generally less than ideal and may have produced substantial fear in regard to heterosexuality, making homosexuality seem so much superior. This will be especially true if the sexual contacts were associated with pain, humiliation, violence, and guilt.

Some homosexuals, male and female, and mostly in their youth, have been exposed to a prejudice against heterosexuality, that it is polluting and dirty; while no such connotations were placed on homosexuality. To be pure, to have never been contaminated by the sexual apparatus of the opposite sex, which usually only occurs in a rather closed gay community, is difficult to overcome however much a person wants to leave homosexual behavior behind.

A woman may greatly fear getting pregnant. Some women are gay due to no other reason than this. Fear of pregnancy can be the result of many factors: improper teaching from a mother, a very unhappy childhood, bad experiences of girlfriends, and so. Nor are these apprehensions totally ungrounded. The pain of labor is a very real thing, for many a most traumatic experience. From early childhood, young girls will often be exposed to the trauma of birth as a major topic of conversation. The grisly tales of breach birth, peritonitis, and other horror tales have had an impact on many women. Movies, particularly westerns, depict women dying in childbirth. Medical textbooks may have been studied that show the surgeon, scissors in hand, cutting the perineum to enlarge the vaginal opening. Indeed, there is much justification for the fear of childbirth, not only for lesbians but for all women. Marriage does not necessarily have to mean children, but the potential is there, of course.

A woman may fear the sexual demands placed upon her by a man. In our culture, the male is generally the sexual aggressor and the woman may dread being under the control of a man. Some women may especially be alarmed at men because of the male supremacy ethic that is supposed to characterize the men. A woman does not desire being a doormat and much of the pro-gay propaganda strongly suggests that this is the way most men treat women. In line with this fear is the apprehension of oral and anal sex. Women know that men may request or demand these. A woman from a gay background may be paralyzed by the thought of having a penis placed into her mouth or anus, whether it is done gently or brutally. The fear of the penis can be mentioned in this connection. Years of lesbianism may build into a woman a fear, disinterest, or hatred of the penis. A woman's psychological response to the male sexuality may be extremely negative and severely retard positive sexual response.

Fear of having to emotionally support a man may be as paramount for a woman as it could be for a man. Marriage would seem to a woman with this fear to be almost unbearable, since it would make escape very difficult.

Though gay women do not usually involve themselves with the high number of lovers that many male homosexuals do, still the threat of exposure is present. Such exposure at any time is frightening, but in the midst of marriage, it is worse.

Psychological response is essential to sexual fulfillment. Sex is dreary at best when there is little or no sexual arousal. A woman who has been thoroughly involved in lesbianism may find the muscular, hairy male body to be completely unattractive. Sexual response could be extremely damaged in such a circumstance, and the thought of having to make love to a rough, bony man may be disgusting for many women.

Given the barriers discussed above, and there are many more, it might seem impossible for a gay person to enter into a satisfying marriage whether with a formerly gay person or a heterosexual. Without honest and open communication, of a fearless nature, sexual concerns may not be able to be resolved. Here is the key: being able to talk together about what is really happening—and this without fear and shame. Not easily achieved, but worth it when it is.

FEAR: A SUMMARY

Marriage may not seem to be a live option for some persons coming from a gay background. The list of fears may seem to be an insurmountable barrier to marriage; but these fears can be reduced and even overcome by the gentle understanding of a marriage partner. Marriage should not be seen as a solution to homosexuality. Marriage must not be a means of proving oneself for whatever reason one may feel he has to prove something. Persons who have attempted to use marriage in that way have experienced many difficulties, and very often it has not worked. Marriage is an option, not an answer. The basic solution to dealing with homosexuality lies in decision, therapy, obedience, the grace of Christ, and the support of others. Many hard emotional battles may be endured, but a loving heterosexual marriage may be worth it all.

Marriage can be a joy, a full expression of humanness, an adventure in whole living and loving in a family, and in full view of society. It can be life full of intimacy, sexuality, with a freedom from guilt and shame. It can be enriched by children and grandchildren. Marriage is a tool created by God for the good of His children. It has been blessed and sanctioned by the Giver of all good and perfect gifts.

A THEOLOGY OF MARRIAGE

Sexuality in man is an intended and basic element in creation. God made man and woman, God made sex—these basic tenets of biblical faith form the core of a theology of marriage. Marriage is the context of human sexuality, invented not by man but by God.

MARRIAGE IN GENESIS

In the Bible's opening chapter, it is recorded that God created man male and female. God made the body, genitals and all. He blessed what He had created and said to the first male and female couple, *"Be fruitful and multiply" (Genesis 1:28)*. The Creator had given His human creatures the capacity to engage in sexual relations and invested therein a pleasure that would both encourage and compel them to do so. In addition, if God had not made sex fun, humans would likely have little interest in engaging in it. The animals could engage in sex too, but of the highest order of His creation, God called their sexual union a "one flesh" union. *"Therefore a man leaves his father and his mother and cleaves to his wife, and they become one flesh" (Genesis 2:24).* "One flesh" is not a dissolving of two into one so that the two lose their identity, but one as in a family—a marriage of one man and one woman. This is why anything other than a one-man/one-woman union is neither "one flesh" nor a marriage. Two men cannot biblically be married to one woman, nor can two women be biblically married to one man. Neither do homosexual "marriages" meet the criteria of a biblical marriage. One flesh requires one man married to one woman.

"One flesh," is the Hebrew phrase and in Hebrew that word is echad. God is an echad. He is three in one. A marriage is two in one. God is complete in Himself, Father, Son, and Holy Spirit. Yes, the Triune God fully meets the requirement of *Deuteronomy 6:4: "Hear O Israel: The LORD our God, the LORD is one."* The marriage of a man and a woman is a complete whole, a unity. Two men or two women cannot be a whole.

Jesus confirmed the Genesis account of the one-flesh relationship. Under questioning from the Pharisees on the matter of divorce, Jesus said:

> But from the beginning of creation, "God made them male and female"..."For this reason a man shall leave his father and mother and be joined to his wife, and the two shall become one." So they are no longer two but one. What therefore God has joined together, let not man put asunder.   Mark 10:6-9

Jesus quoted from Genesis 1:27 and Genesis 2:24. Both statements sequentially come before the fall of man, that rebellion of the first humans against their Creator, yet Jesus does not refer to that fall but demonstrates that the original intent of God stands throughout history regardless of man's sinful state. He verifies the sexuality of man in terms of male and female, and the naturalness of their sexual relations. The way Jesus quoted Genesis 1:27 and Genesis 2:24 indicates clearly that basic sexuality, in terms of biology, was for the purpose of sexual intercourse. We observe by the quotation from Genesis by Jesus that marriage is foundational in both the Old and New Testament.

God did not make man a sexual being strictly for the purpose of procreation. God made woman for man, because without her, man was incomplete: *"Then the Lord God said, 'It is not good that the man should be alone; I will make him a helper fit for him'"* (Genesis 2:23a). The first man Adam, a "person," did not find in all the rest of creation another "person" until he met the first woman. Man, created in the image of God, special and distinct from all other flesh, is uniquely person. Adam was not to be person alone; he was lonely until he was "wed" to another person who could complement him. The male and female persons together could reproduce themselves as part of a natural biological function, and they could also be "help" to one another.

The first couple was naked, yet the carnal consciousness of that was not reality to them. They existed in a sexual paradise, free to love each other in joyful desire, pure and simple. They beheld one another's bodies in exuberant innocence. It was not until the fall that they even recognized themselves to be naked (compare Genesis 2:25 and Genesis 3:7). It is evident from the Genesis account that sexuality was immediately impacted by sin. We are left to speculate as to why that was so, but it may be that sexuality is so central to the core of our being that it was inevitably damaged when sin collided with immaculate simplicity.

Christ has redeemed us and is in the process of freeing us from the consequences of disobedience. Though we cannot entirely reenter the primeval paradise and enjoy the free sexuality humans once knew, we can live with the intention of God for our lives in regard to sexuality and enjoy the abundance of love and pleasure God has placed there. This means submission to God's plan for sex, by observing the commands for sexual expression and by allowing His grace to infiltrate our loving. If God's agape love is absent from our relationships, it results in a limitation of the love we experience. Perfect loving and sexuality can be experienced only as God's agape love is infused into the one-flesh marriage. The physical act is simply one aspect of sex. The spirit of man, when energized by Spirit and agape, is capable of transcending the animal level of sensation and moving to a more genuine level of human sexuality.

Love is the giving of oneself. We see this most vividly in the incarnation (the Word become flesh) and especially in Jesus' death on the cross. In God's sexuality, the entire person is given to another in sexual union. Eve was given to Adam by the Creator; they, two persons, became one flesh. Their sexual union was the deepest and most meaningful of all their interpersonal relationships. That relationship established a mutual knowledge and dependence from which there could be no satisfactory break. This is why the ideal marriage is to be permanent.

A marriage is a joining. Each culture has its mechanism by which a marriage is identified. In Eden there was no one else observing, so God did the joining. In the world today there is considerable conformity regarding marriage. The observance of communal requirements for marriage, though they may vary, nevertheless are determinative of what is a legitimate marriage.

MARRIAGE AND THE COMMANDS

The commands regarding sexuality and marriage reveal the power of sexual union. One flesh is an extraordinary reality. The sexual coming together of two people in the context of marriage establishes the strongest of bonds. This is why marriage is safeguarded by commands. The seventh commandment is, *"You shall not commit adultery" (Exodus 20:14).* That basic command is upheld by the Psalmist and the prophets. Jesus upheld it. He included adultery and fornication in a list of sins that defile persons (Matthew 15:19). In addition, He expanded the act of adultery to include the lustful desiring of another (Matthew 5:27-28).

Paul recognized the commands of Scripture and endorsed God's plan of sexuality. Perhaps the most relevant passage is the one in which Paul includes homosexuality in a list of sins. In I Corinthians 6:9, he speaks of *"the immoral," "adulterers," and "homosexuals."* Every category of sexual deviance is covered by these three terms. In Galatians 5:19, Paul speaks of *"immorality, impurity, licentiousness,"* and says these are works of the flesh (of rebellion) as opposed to fruit of the Spirit. In Colossians 3:5, Paul says, *"Put to death therefore what is earthly in you: immorality, impurity, passion, evil desires."* These are the four false loves, four ways that love can be distorted.

The commands of Scripture tell us of God's intention and purpose. At the same time, they lift up the status of marriage. God has surrounded His truth with a high fence. It is a clear standard that cannot be avoided, or rejected, by the whim of those who desire to authenticate sinful behavior.

MARRIAGE: CHRIST AND THE CHURCH

Marriage reflects the joining of Christ and His Church. A husband is to love his wife and be willing to lay down his life for her. A wife is to respect and submit to her husband; she is to love him. Paul says this and much more in Ephesians 5:22–33. The husband is the head of the wife, as Christ is the head of the church. As the church is submissive or subject to Christ, so wives are to be subject to their husbands. Husbands are to love their wives as Christ loved the church and gave Himself up for her. A husband is to nourish and cherish his wife as Christ does the church. As a husband and wife become one, so Christ and the church are one. Paul says it is all a great mystery, but he takes it *"to mean Christ and the church" (Ephesians 5:32).*

Jesus came to build His church. This is the essence of the kingdom of God. Christ died for the church; it is God's church. There is nothing more central to Scripture. And marriage is analogous to Christ and the church. There is no more lofty expression of marriage in the Bible. It is more sublime than words will admit. John Calvin wrote: "Christ has been pleased to put such honor upon marriage, as to make it an image of his sacred union with the Church. What could be said more, in commendation of the dignity of marriage?"

MARRIAGE IS HONORABLE

The writer of Hebrews exhorts, *"Let marriage be held in honor among all" (Hebrews 13:4).* This is a fitting conclusion to all the foregoing. Though marriage has suffered greatly at the hands of us sinners, still it is at the heart of God's plan for sexuality for His people during their pilgrimage in this age. We must not allow divorces and bad marriages to deter us from honoring marriage. Since marriage is in the mainstream concern of God, then He will help us cope with the fears and bad experiences that might easily dissuade us from a commitment to a person of the opposite sex. The Lord does restore and repair that which was overthrown and destroyed.

MARRIAGE: PART OF OUR PILGRIMAGE

Though normal for our living and vigorously upheld in the Scriptures, marriage is not the final state of things. It exists now for us earth-bound creatures. It will pass away one day as something that has served its purpose but is no longer needed. We learn this from Jesus when, in reference to life in the kingdom of God, He said, *"For in the resurrection they neither marry nor are given in marriage, but are like angels in heaven" (Matthew 22:30).*

ASEXUALITY AND CELIBACY

Martin Luther prayed:

> O Lord, if it is thy divine will that I should live without a wife, then help me to do so! If not, bestow upon me a good, pious maid, with whom I can live my whole life long, one whom I love and who loves me.

How many courageous and hopeful people from a gay background have prayed a similar prayer! If not a conscious prayer, then at least it was a silent but powerful cry out of the depths of being. We are sexual beings; we are made to be loved and to love. It is part of how we have been created. Yet, for many reasons, whether tragic, necessary, or chosen, many of God's children embrace asexuality and celibacy.

There is a difference between asexuality and celibacy. *The Random House Dictionary of the English Language* (1973 edition) defines "asexual" as: "1. not sexual. 2. having no sex or sexual organs. 3. independent of sexual processes." The same dictionary defines "celibacy" as: "1. state of being unmarried. 2. abstention by vow from marriage e.g., the celibacy of priests. 3. abstention from sexual relations."

ASEXUALITY

The primary difference between asexuality and celibacy is that celibacy is generally a choice; asexuality is determined by circumstances. A person emerging from a homosexual background may be asexual. Having turned his/her back on homosexuality, they are left in an asexual place. Cutting off the gay life may result in an immediate loss in concern for sex of any kind, so it is as though their sexual organs had been removed or their body refuses to produce the standard sexual hormones. It may be temporary, due mostly to psychological processes. It may be permanent. A person in this situation has not chosen to be asexual; rather, asexuality has descended upon him/her. Often upon conversion to Jesus Christ, a person will experience temporary asexuality much as a converted drug addict will undergo a complete alleviation of the need for drugs. This is generally temporary. In my years of working in the drug culture in San Francisco, I have observed what I believe is God's removing a person's dependence on drugs for a period of time, so the person has a chance to be grounded in a new way of life. Certainly, psychological factors are operating as well, but the Spirit is also involved. However, a person who has experienced the loss of his/her sex drive has not made a vow of celibacy. He/she has not made a determination to abstain from sexual relations. But a celibate has.

It is not a sin to be asexual. It is better to suffer the loss of one's sexual drive than to be driven by carnal lusts and never be free to live a normal life. I believe it is possible for God to remove either permanently or temporarily one's sex drive for their own benefit. On the other hand, a person may simply but severely reject their sexuality, seeking a sense of relief from the distorted sex drive that has been destroying their life. Relevant here are Jesus' words in *Mark 9:43, "And if your hand causes you to sin, cut it off; it is better for you to enter life maimed than with two hands to go to hell, to the unquenchable fire."* This is, of course, to be taken spiritually rather than literally. It is not the hand that must be dealt with; rather, it is the will and spirit of a person that must be tamed. For many people in "normal" heterosexuality, this may seem extreme but persons from a gay background will quickly grasp the impact of the foregoing. In any event, a period of sexual neutrality can be a precious gift to many. Asexuality, if due to a psychological and/or spiritual process, may be temporary and celibacy may become a live option for asexual persons at a later point.

CELIBACY

Celibacy is an honorable state. The ancient Greeks thought so because of their dualistic concept of the universe in which spirit and reason were good and matter (especially the flesh) was evil. Sexuality then, fleshly as it would appear, was evil while celibacy was admired. Historically, homosexuality often thrived under such circumstances because it was viewed as superior to heterosexuality and not seen as fleshly.

God did make us male and female and did establish marriage; He has made us capable of living in a married relationship. However, this does not mean that every person is bound to live in the married state.

Jesus did not marry, and Paul, regardless of whether he had been previously married, did not live in the marital state during his apostolate. Their lives were lived in the presence of the kingdom of God, under the shadow of the eschaton—in Jesus' case, the cross, and in Paul's, the second coming of Christ and the end of the age. Their circumstances may not be normative, but they are not beyond the range of contemporary possibility. Both Jesus and Paul demonstrated a life of fulfillment and purpose apart from marriage. Yet, neither taught that celibacy was superior to marriage.

EUNUCHS AND CELIBATES

Matthew 19:11-12 contains a key understanding of celibacy.

> *Not all men can receive this precept, but only those to whom it is given. For there are eunuchs who have been so from birth, and there are eunuchs who have been made eunuchs by men, and there are eunuchs who have made themselves eunuchs for the sake of the kingdom of heaven.*

In context, Jesus had been teaching on divorce. He had stated that when a married person divorces and marries another, this person commits adultery. (Some contend that divorce is not forgivable, but that view runs counter to the doctrine of grace. Divorce, not the intent of God and always the result of sin, does not bar a person from the cleansing blood of Jesus.) The disciples, stunned by Jesus' words, respond with a form of exaggeration and protest that perhaps it would be better never to marry. Jesus responds by saying, *"Not all men can receive this precept, but only those to whom it is given"* (Matthew 19:11).

Jesus said that voluntary celibacy was a gift. A gift from whom? it may be asked. Probably, though not explicitly, it is a gift from God. This is an important issue for that one who desires celibacy. Is there a "gift"?

The idea of a gift is also expressed by Paul in his first letter to the Corinthians. In dealing with marriage and the sexual relations therein, he lets those believers in Corinth know that he wishes they were much less concerned with sex and marriage than they are. He wishes they were like he is—single and therefore free to serve Christ (see 1 Corinthians 7:6-7). He concludes, though, by saying in verse 7,

"But each has his own special gift from God, one of one kind and one of another."

In Matthew 19:11, the word for gift is the common verb used in normal situations where something is given. But in 1 Corinthians 7:7, Paul uses the word "charisma" or grace gift, a word used to convey that God is the giver. This is the word used in 1 Corinthians 12:4 and Romans 12:6 to describe gifts of the Holy Spirit. Paul then sees voluntary celibacy as a gift given by God. John Calvin looked upon continence, the controlling of the sexual urge, as "a special gift bestowed upon very few, and only those who have been appointed by God can endure the sacrifices of the celibate life."

Getting back to Matthew 19:12, we see there are three classes of eunuchs or celibates. (Technically, eunuchs are men who lack testicles but who can still have an erection and engage in sexual intercourse. However, it is my opinion that Jesus has in mind here all persons of both sexes, especially those in the third class below, who abstain from sex.) First, there are persons who are incapable of a sex life because of nature—either they do not have the physical ability or they are not capable of sexual excitement. Second, some persons have been made incapable of having a sex life, having been castrated, sterilized, or somehow otherwise maimed with the result that sex is out of the question. Third, there are people who have voluntarily chosen to silence, repress, or sublimate their sex drive and have determined not to marry for the sake of their work on behalf of the kingdom of God. Jesus admonished His hearers that, *"He who is able to receive this, let him receive it,"* meaning that some could not. Others could receive it and would do so. Jesus Himself received it. Perhaps He knew He was going to the cross and so wanted to spare a wife that scandal and bereavement. He also knew that He needed to give His all to the huge task before Him. Paul likewise chose to live as a single man for the cause of Christ. This especially is seen in 1 Corinthians 7:8, 25–31. For Paul, the kingdom was at hand, and he determined to put all his time, energy, and love into it. It was no sin to marry (verse 28), but he taught that in light of the approach of the great day of the Lord and the "impending distress," it would be better not to marry.

Jesus did not refer to His second coming or to any persecution in Matthew 19:12. Unconditionally, He lifted celibacy up as an honorable life. It seems He felt there would be few who could receive celibacy, but in any case, it could be authentically chosen for the sake of the kingdom of heaven.

FURTHER BIBLICAL MATERIAL ON CELIBACY

Though not explicitly dealing with celibacy, Mark 10:29–30 implicitly treats it. Jesus is proclaiming the radical decision the rich must make in order to enter the kingdom. Jesus said that everyone who has renounced possessions, persons, and other commitments for His sake and the gospel would receive it all back, a hundredfold now and in the age to come, eternal life. Voluntarily choosing celibacy would fit here.

Many former homosexuals will never be heterosexual, and celibacy may be a blessed answer for them. Jesus promises reward, although what form it might take is difficult to determine from the biblical text. However, it could take many beautiful forms. Ideally, it may be in the context of His Church, where a single person has brothers and sisters, mothers and fathers, sons and daughters. For instance, Paul had a son in Timothy. God's church is intended to be a family.

In Luke 14:26, Jesus lifts discipleship up to an extraordinarily high position. This is the controversial passage on "hating" mother, wife, children, brothers, and sisters. A decision to be celibate for the kingdom of God can be viewed as an element of discipleship and, as such, has Jesus' blessing.

Isaiah has a stunning word from the Lord on celibacy:

> *For thus says the Lord: "To the eunuchs who keep my Sabbaths, who choose the things that please me and hold fast my covenant, I will give in my house and within my walls a monument and a name better than sons and daughters; I will give them an everlasting name which shall not be cut off."*   Isaiah 56:4-5

Probably the eunuchs Isaiah writes of are castrated men, but the spiritual reality for men and women celibates stands nevertheless. Though the celibate will not have children, he/she will be compensated by God with a place in the kingdom of God, compensated or rewarded with an everlasting name that will not be cut off. This is a high promise from God.

REFLECTIONS ON CELIBACY

Celibacy need not be a permanent state. It may be that considerable healing may occur for a person while he/she is unmarried and abstaining from sexual relationships. Persons from a gay background who opt for celibacy for the sake of the kingdom, and/or because there is no other righteous alternative, may be in a state at some point where marriage is possible or desirable. Celibacy is far better than continuing in sin, whether that be homosexual or heterosexual sinful behavior.

Celibacy is best when the sex drive is effectively sublimated, that is channeled into a living enterprise such as art, music, drama, writing, sports, serving the poor, and much more. However, a person may be unmarried and masturbate. Although this is largely a controversial topic, I feel that controlled or moderate self-stimulation is acceptable and healthy. A person who is asexual would not masturbate, but a celibate has that option open to him/her. I see masturbation in a neutral position. It certainly has a destructive side. I have counseled people who engaged in masturbation up to eight times a day. This slavery is not the freedom Christ promises us. Masturbation can be used to avoid interaction with other people. The person who says, in effect, "I don't need anybody" and who is fulfilled through masturbation may be suffering from a narcissistic complex that will cut off all growth and leave him/her with a warped and twisted personality. However, if masturbation serves as a genuine release and does not produce a drive to fulfill sexual fantasies, it may not be sin. Sexual responsibility should be everyone's goal. If masturbation cannot be controlled and approached in a rational, ordered, calculated, and non-emotional manner, then it should be avoided. An additional danger of masturbation is that it sets up a conditioning pattern for an orgasm. A person becomes accustomed to responding to a set pattern and there can be problems in adjusting to real intercourse.

Though Paul describes celibacy as a charismatic gift and Jesus indicated it may be hard to receive, celibacy will arise out of a person's will. It is a decision. This is not to preclude the work of the Holy Spirit, but a person's "I decide" is essential. What I mean is, celibacy may not be a gift at first. It may be a struggle, a question of continual battles, some won and some lost. It may be that God would bless with special grace the person who steps out on faith and decides for celibacy. In fact, I believe this is how it does work. Rather than being an instantaneous act of God, the gift of celibacy is given in response to faith. It is the manifestation of God honoring our sacrificial decision for His glory. The obedient resolution to follow God's commands stirs up the grace of God toward the believer. Anyone desiring the celibate life must exercise faith and begin to trust Christ whether the explicit gift is obvious or not.

A special concern though comes to mind: What of the person who, despite all, continually fails at controlling the sexual drive? This is probably the more common circumstance; the sex drive is powerful, and if it were not, humans would have long ago become extinct. We are neither failures, nor hopeless sinners, if we fight and fail. Real faith keeps getting up and trying again.

The love of a man or woman is a wonderful thing, but it is not the all in all. There is no human relationship that does not have in it some conflict and pain. Those who have voluntarily or involuntarily found their life is one of celibacy need not lead a loveless life. The love of Jesus surpasses all loves. Some of the greatest saints of the church who were celibates, such as Theresa of Avila, St. Francis of Assisi, St. John of the Cross, Brother Lawrence, and many more, experienced lives full of love. Jesus is the lover of our souls. The Song of Solomon portrays such love. The relationships of David and Jonathan, Ruth and Naomi, and Paul and Timothy reveal purity of love and devotion seldom seen in marriages. Intimacy need not always necessitate sexuality. Commitment, involvement, close loving friendships are open to the celibate, and perhaps more readily available because sex does not have to enter the picture. Sex and the sex drive can build walls and destroy friendships. Celibacy has much to offer as a starting place for building strong relationships.

Richard Rohr, O.F.M., is a pastor of the New Jerusalem Community in Cincinnati, Ohio. He wrote an article for Sojourners entitled, "Reflections on Marriage and Celibacy," in which he referred to the increase in people who are deciding for celibacy. He wrote:

> We are seeing the gift arise quite naturally among some of our most healthy and receptive members in the community. It is not tied to any sense of ministry, efficiency, or "victims offering," but appears to be a deep word of truth that is heard in the context of personal prayer and real sharing. It is a sense of vocation and integrity which, like all prophetic actions, has a

hard time explaining itself or justifying itself to anyone else—and often even to the individual who has chosen it. It is an absolute newness which says that God is sufficient, but it is also an absolute solitude which says the world is lonely and passing away.

Celibacy is neither inferior to nor superior to marriage. The commitment to celibacy leaves open the possibility of either continued celibacy or marriage.

2

Factors of Change

MOVING TOWARD THE POSSIBILITY OF MARRIAGE

Persons can change, and even their sexual orientation can be transformed. This book is based on this concept. It is not a process of reconditioning, that is, using a methodology of reward and punishment to get a person to be stimulated by the opposite rather than the same sex.

Radical change in terms of basic sexual identity has been thought nearly impossible. Sex-change surgery that is carried on to such a large degree now exemplifies this. Transsexual surgery points up a kind of hopelessness. But there is always hope. The knife and plastic surgery do not have to be the only answer.

Perry Desmond, formally known in New Orleans as "The South's Most Beautiful Boy," had a sex-change operation. He was castrated and shot full of female hormones. Some time later, he became a Christian. After growing and struggling, Perry regained his natural identity. Though the operation could not be completely reversed, Perry rejected his attempt to be a woman and became the man he once was, but this time as choice and not by compulsion. Perry wrote a book about his experience. He called it, *Perry: A Transformed Transsexual*.[1]

Perry's story tells me that homosexuals are not born, they are made. There is increasing evidence that this is so. Studies by Masters and Johnson show the same. It is not fixed as skin color is; change is possible. A person may actually be a "former homosexual" or "ex-gay."

It is the "how" of change that is the chief concern of this chapter.

---

1   Perry Desmond and Robert L. Hymers, *Perry: A Transformed Transsexual* (Tronton, MO: Metamorphis Books, 1978).

Our source is two-fold. One, we have the Bible and theological principles that stem from a study of the Bible. Two, we have experience, primarily the experiences of many who have become former homosexuals. These two will be blended to present a reason, a hope, and a possibility for people who, coming from a gay background, are moving toward marriage.

THE BIBLICAL AND THEOLOGICAL GROUNDS FOR CHANGE

God is almighty; He is the creator of all things. He made humans special and has a special love for them. His Son became human. God is omnipotent, and the worst sinners become great saints through His changing power. The lives of Mary Magdalene and Paul reveal the transforming power of Jesus. No person is ever too far away or is too great a sinner for God to love. In my years of ministry, I've seen grace and mercy extended to homosexual prostitutes, transsexuals, child molesters, gay pornographic film actors and actresses, leathermen, and more. God's basic posture is that He is *"not wishing that any should perish, but that all should reach repentance"* (2 Peter 3:9).

CONVERSION

There are many types of conversion. One can be converted to a political philosophy or to a natural food diet. One can be converted to communism or capitalism, from heterosexuality to homosexuality and vice versa. Christian conversion, though similar to other conversions in terms of psychological and sociological processes, is different in that it is change brought about by the Holy Spirit. An analyst of conversions, including Christian conversion, could define underlying influences that made a person open to conversion, but could not discern the spiritual work of God that goes on in the "inner man."

Conversion is almost impossible to talk about with any real confidence. Conversion to Christ is so much a work of the Holy Spirit that it seems almost beyond our understanding. My view of conversion is that it is all of God. A general breakdown of conversion looks like this: One, God convicts us of our sin. Two, God shows us that we are incapable of achieving our own righteousness, that we are in fact, lost, condemned, and hopeless. Three, we now have an interest in Jesus; we gain an attraction to Him as Savior. Four, conversion occurs, the greatest of all miracles, of which we are not in control. Five, we begin growing up into the stature of the fullness of Christ. This fifth stage of conversion is known theologically as sanctification, and a big part of this is repentance. Repentance is a slow process, perhaps continuing throughout our entire lives. If any of us would have to have repented of all our sin in order to be converted, well, that would not happen. I have the sense that if I had been presented with all my sinning before my conversion and that conversion would not happen without my ability to repent of it all, then it would have been a barrier far too much for me. Another part of sanctification is learning to trust Jesus, to have faith in Jesus as we live our lives.

REPENTANCE

Repentance is a major Biblical theme. It is essentially a change of mind, which then leads to a change in behavior. The basic repenting is to turn to Jesus as Savior and Lord, rather than to turn away from Him. Repentance is a work of God in the life of the born from above person; in our own strength we are completely incapable of it.

The gay person will rightly think of his/her homosexuality first when hearing the word repent. There must be a change in regard to homosexual behavior. We must agree with the Bible on this very key point. Paul said in 1 Corinthians 6:9–10 that homosexuals will not inherit the kingdom of God. This must be taken seriously by anyone wanting freedom from homosexuality. Motivation to repent must come from a desire to follow Christ and please God. Some persons have repented of sorts from homosexuality because of the problems it presented, such as severe trauma, and so they desired to "get their hand off the hot stove." Others have come to a place of ambivalence. Knowing right from wrong, they desire change, yet they are unwilling to pay the costs of a deep commitment. Inadvertently, they have arrived at the most unrewarding position of all: knowing the truth yet continuing in sin. This situation produces destruction in body, mind, and spirit. Half-way repentance is frustrating at best. Repentance must be for more than survival, comfort, and convenience. It must be God-directed.

There are three elements in repentance. The first is the intellectual element. This means that repentance involves a changing of the mind, the admitting of sins. The Greek word for repentance, metanoia, means a changing of the mind. A person must consciously acknowledge that he or she is wrong and that God is right. It is our pride that must be battled here. This is especially difficult for the gay person who has closely identified with the "gay pride" emphasis and the sophistication adopted by many homosexuals.

The second element is emotional. This involves a feeling of sorrow for sin. But this is not a sorrow about the trouble sin has produced, but a sorrow brought on by the knowledge that we have sinned against God and others. A secondary Greek word for repentance in the New Testament, *metamelomai*, emphasizes the caring element in repentance.[2] Paul said, *"For godly grief produces a repentance that leads to salvation and brings no regret, but worldly grief produces death"* (2 Corinthians 7:10).

The third element involves decision; it is the volitional element. The emphasis here is on a change of will, a genuine decision to turn from sin. A person can intellectually repent of sin and can feel sorrow for it, but he or she must decide to cease sinful behavior. By our own will we must decide, "I turn from my sin now." This does not mean the sin issue has been determined once and for all. We are yet sinners. But now there is a struggle against sin and no longer a willing compliance to it. We must be willing; it is with the will that God works. His Holy Spirit meets us right there and helps us. The divine-human interchange happens in a way that we do not understand. Paul referred to this dynamic relationship when he said, *"For this I toil, striving with all the energy which he mightily inspires within me"* (Colossians 1:29). As a person with a gay orientation struggles against the pull of homosexuality; God is at work giving grace and strength for the battle.

Repentance, when it is thorough, brings significant healing to a person. Normally, a homosexual thinks of the sexual act as the sinful part, and that is obviously true. However, there are other considerations. Certainly, a person cannot help the gay tendency once it is fully entrenched in the psyche. It may be a long while before that tendency is removed, or perhaps it will never be completely gone. The sinful sexual act must be repented of, but repentance can go deeper. There is the matter of the lustful fantasies, that for some have been so much a part of the whole lifestyle., Then there are the parents, friends,

---

2   See Matthew 21:29–32, 27:3; 2 Corinthians 7:8.

husbands, wives, and children who have been affected. And at a deep level is the rebellion against God, the rebellion against self, and any other abuses that must be dealt with before repentance can have its total beneficial way in a person's life.

We repent and God forgives. It is the world's best deal. The Scripture says, *"If we confess our sins, he is faithful and just, and will forgive our sins and cleanse us from all unrighteousness"* (1 John 1:9).

Paul's terrifying statement about homosexuals and other sinners found in 1 Corinthians 6:9–10 is followed by these incredible words: *"And such were some of you. But you were washed, you were sanctified, you were justified in the name of the Lord Jesus Christ and in the Spirit of our God."*

FAITH

Faith may be expressed as trust, reliance upon, or obedience. It is being dependent on God.

The Bible abundantly testifies to the importance of faith. We are saved by faith (Acts 16:31 and Ephesians 2:8), kept safe in Christ by faith (Romans 11:20, 2 Corinthians 1:24, 1 Peter 1:5, and 1 John 5:4), healed by faith (James 5:15 and Acts 14:9), walk by faith (2 Corinthians 5:7), and we overcome problems by faith (Mark 9:23, Romans 4:18–21, and Hebrews 11:17–19). Faith is necessary to please God (Hebrews 11:6), and without it, God's power is limited in our lives (Mark 6:2–6).

As in repentance, there are three parts to faith: the intellectual, emotional, and volitional elements. Each of these is something that God works into our lives; we are utterly incapable of achieving them, try as we might. The Holy Spirit, indwelling us, grows us up, and works His will into our lives.

First, there is something concrete to believe. Paul says that if we confess with our mouth that *"Jesus is Lord"* and believe in our hearts that God has raised Him from the dead, then we will be saved (see Romans 10:9). The Holy Spirit will make it clear to us that Jesus did die for our sin, that we can be forgiven of our sin through His death on the cross, and that He was raised from the dead. We will see and believe in our minds that Jesus is the Christ, the Savior, God become flesh. We will understand and believe that we are separated from God because of our sin and that Jesus reconciles us to the Father.

The second element of faith is emotional. This refers to a trusting with the heart, the feeling, and empathizing aspect of our being. Paul said, *"For man believes with this heart and so is justified"* (Romans 10:10a). The "heart" here is used figuratively to refer to the center or seat of our emotions. Faith involves a heartfelt giving of ourselves to the Lord Jesus. It may be a small feeling, just a very little bit of emotion, but it is a giving of our being to God.

The third element is volitional. It is a willing desire to follow Jesus as Savior and Lord. We cannot see Jesus in the flesh, but even so, we desire Him to be our Savior. Jesus asks us to give up everything to follow Him.

God is the source of faith; faith is a gift of God. First, He convicts us of sin, then He shows us the covering for our sin, Jesus Christ, and finally, He helps us "accept" His Son. We receive even faith, the faith to accept Jesus as the Christ.

Faith is directed believing. Jesus Christ, His person and work, is the object of faith. Faith is not a leap into darkness; it is a leap to Christ.

Faith is retaining truth, clinging to it despite everything. C. S. Lewis said of it, "Now faith ... is the act of holding on to things your reason has once accepted, in spite of your changing moods."[3]

A NEW SECURITY SYSTEM

It has helped me to think of the Christian life as the learning and growing into a new security system. The Christian life is counting on Christ rather than our own abilities. We are not to inordinately disparage ourselves, but we are not to believe that we and we alone are above all things and need only ourselves to experience fullness of life both here and in eternity. Often sin is simply a way of coping with the harsh realities of living. Much sin we would not commit if we knew how not to. A person from a gay background knows exactly what I mean. It is love that is sought, not merely sex. It is affection that is needed; it is acceptance and understanding that a person hungers for. When those needs and desires are increasingly met by Christ and His Church, the vices and devices formerly needed for the sake of survival begin to fade away. It is a process in learning that Jesus can make a significant

---

3   C. S. Lewis, *Mere Christianity* (New York: Macmillan Publishing Co., Inc., 1943), p. 123.

difference, that His way, although difficult, is far better.

Christianity is all-encompassing; it applies to all areas of life. It is grown into, little by little. There are hot spots, depressions, plateaus, backslidings, tremendous growth spurts, bruised knees, and scars. It is a life that works, a new security system, the lifestyle originally designed for us.

A NEW IDENTITY

A newness breaks into our lives at conversion. It is that intangible something, a mystery that no analyst can grasp. The homosexual is no longer homosexual, though homosexual desires will no doubt still be present. The liar is no longer a liar, though he may still lie.

It is not uncommon for gay people to be proud of their homosexuality. Being a homosexual provides an identity; it is a way of being different. This pride may only be a kind of bravado that compensates for strong feelings of inferiority, but it can be a rigid identity. All Christians have left behind some kind of identity to become followers of Jesus and have found greater liberty in their new identity. Christ and the life He has for us is a rich life and secure identity. In time there can be a transfer of identity from being a homosexual to being a Christian.

By God's Spirit, genuine conversion places each of us into Christ. Paul says we are a new creature (2 Corinthians 5:17); we are made new in Christ. All the problems have not been cleared up, but from God's point of view, we are saints. A gay person who trusts Christ as Savior can break out of the homosexual label. It is not adopting a heterosexual label, but rather it is identifying with Christ. We are Christians over, above, and against anything else.

PERSEVERANCE

Courage is required to live the Christian life. It is on the one hand a simple life, but on the other hand, it is difficult. Rejection is one of the major problems. Most gays faced heavy rejection in their formative years. Perhaps they had parents who were unloving or indifferent, plus peers who belittled, scorned, and were openly hostile to them. For most, the process of arriving at a secure identity in homosexuality was far from easy. Now, conversion to Christ brings a new wave of rejection, this time from those very people who rescued the gay person from the rejection of the straight community. It is no wonder, then, that the new Christian attempts to keep some of the security offered by the gay world. The gay church, e.g., the Metropolitan Community Church, tries to have Christ and gayness, too. It appeals to many who desire religion in their lives but who are unwilling or feel they are unable to give up their homosexual identity. The gay church is the church of compromise and a deadly one in the light of 1 Corinthians 6:9–11 and 1 John 3:4–6; 2:1–6, 15–17. Christ was not being arbitrary when He said that we cannot serve two masters, that we must choose between God and mammon (Matthew 6:24). Nor was John being critical when he wrote of certain individuals saying that *"they loved the praise of men more than the praise of God"* (John 12:43). It is a tough decision for a person to set themselves apart from a community that has accepted, supported, and comforted them, perhaps for many years. Often, gay people build their whole lives in a gay context. It is possible to live completely within the gay world and never leave it. Expulsion from that world makes one an alien. The risks involved in conversion for a gay person are high. They will need the loving support of a new family.

Leaving a gay world may mean financial ruin. Many gay people are tied up in business and property ownership with lovers or former lovers. For a homosexual to turn to Christ may mean complete financial bankruptcy.

In general, the gay world is more sexually oriented than the straight world, especially for the younger gay in the street scene. Following Jesus will mean a turning from that sexual involvement and will mean the possibility that, at least for a time, sex will disappear from one's life. The thought of no more sex can be a highly disturbing one.

It will take great courage for most homosexually oriented people to follow Jesus. It will require perseverance. Perseverance is the steady persistence in a course of action, the continuing in the grace of God until the gift of salvation is consummated in heaven. It is doggedly clinging to Christ despite everything that may happen.

The believer is not alone in the battle. Paul wrote, *"... for God is at work in you, both to will and to work for his good pleasure"* (Philippians 2:13). The Holy Spirit dwells in and with the Christian, working to bring about the will of God. It is not simply a question of a person's will over against the world, the flesh, and the devil.

In Romans 8:35, Paul asks this rhetorical question, *"Who shall separate us from the love of Christ?"* He then proceeds to mention every possible disaster known to man, every fear and danger, every demon and power, and he concludes that the believer is very safe in Christ. In fact, in all of the creation, there is nothing that can tear us loose from God. But God's tremendous keeping power and our perseverance go together. We are secure in Christ, even if we were to stumble and fall. God will bring His children back and restore them.

HOPE

Hope is a beautiful word. There will be some, who in the process of turning away from homosexual behavior, who will marry, others will never try, and others will try and not succeed. Some may go back into the gay life. But hope is still present. Bible hope is for the present and for the future, hope now and then—hope now because Christ is making us new; hope then because we will one day be with Jesus in His kingdom. This means a great deal for anyone who takes eternity seriously and realizes the transitory nature of our life on this planet. Romans 15:13 has the expression of hope that excites me that most. It reads, *"May the God of hope fill you with all joy and peace in believing, so that by the power of the Holy Spirit you may abound in hope."*

A TIME FOR HONESTY

To move from a homosexual lifestyle to heterosexual marriage is an incredibly dramatic event. This is not a book of easy answers or empty promises; my personal life experience shows me there are no simple solutions and my work with ex-gays vividly illustrates the trauma of walking away from a homosexual orientation. Honesty is an absolute necessity in the life of a person wanting to leave the gay life behind.

ADMITTING THE STRUGGLE

Sometimes, persons undergo a dramatic and sudden conversion, leaving them with a genuine sense of freedom from sexual desire. One day they are ready for any sexual encounter and the next, they are ready to be abstinent forever! However, usually the sex drive returns after a period of time. God "takes the pressure off" for a time, but later, He allows life to return to normal. If the return of the sex drive of the new believer is not honestly dealt with, there will be major problems ahead.

If a person is lustful, he/she is helped by admitting it. Denying it for the sake of keeping up appearances will do harm. It is much better to bring the reality of what is confronting us out into the open. "Ventilating," as psychology has amply demonstrated, is very helpful. Being able to talk about it to others who can empathize, comfort, and pray about this problem is a valuable resource. It is extremely important for people to be honest about what is happening in their lives.

Psychic response is almost impossible to eliminate. "Psychic response" means sexual arousal by the sight of (or thought of) another person. Of course, heterosexuals have this too; you cannot prevent psychic response. However, you can avoid taking it any further. The first step in dealing with psychic response is to admit that it exists. Psychic response is not sinful, although it can be a prelude to sin. In being honest with yourself about temptation can mean bringing it in prayer to God. It is healthy to have the kind of prayer life that allows for flowing, open communication. Speak to a friend about the lustful thought or the arousal you feel that is so difficult to withstand. Honesty here is a sign of strength and good sense; covering up is dangerous. The power of psychic response, its intensity, and even its frequency, will diminish with every "No!" Victory over it comes when we stand against it and refuse to let it become part of our thoughts or actions.

PUTTING ASIDE OLD PATTERNS

The homosexual lifestyle is all-encompassing. Every aspect of life is affected. Breaking free from the gay life necessitates throwing idols and accompanying paraphernalia into the fire (this may be taken quite literally in some circumstances). The demand for honesty at this point is essential. The decision to walk away from homosexuality, and especially to make the move toward marriage, means a confronting of old patterns with the intent of casting out anything that is ungodly and unhealthy.

LOVERS

Lovers are people who may have meant a great deal in terms of love, sex, communication, intimacy, and friendship. They are people who made life seem a little less threatening. Lovers are not easy to let go of and will probably never be forgotten. But for the former homosexual, past lovers must always remain in the past. Perhaps they may remain friends, but often this is not possible. Past lovers must sometimes be excluded from one's life in a radical kind of way because the temptations they represent may be too hard to resist. An ex-lover, feeling threatened by a Christian choice, may strenuously seek to undo the conversion by cajoling, taunting, belittling, and intimidation. They can make ultimatums and generally bring coercion about in a myriad of ways. It is necessary to throw away the address books and the phone numbers, not clinging to them "just in case." Gifts from former lovers may also have to be discarded, sold, or given away.

It is heart breaking, mentally excruciating, and spiritually draining to walk away from lovers. Such conflict is not unusual for the Christian, since we are called to *"count everything as loss because of the surpassing worth of knowing Christ Jesus my Lord."* Paul amplified on that statement recorded in Philippians 3:8 by adding, *"For his sake I have suffered the loss of all things, and count them as refuse, in order that I may gain Christ."*

We can count on the fact that God is aware of our struggle. It is not unreasonable that the cost of following Christ is high. Jesus did promise,

> *"Truly, I say to you, there is no one who has left house or brothers or sisters or mother or father or children or lands, for my sake and for the gospel, who will not receive a hundredfold now in this time, houses and brothers and sisters and mothers and children and lands, with persecutions, and in the age to come eternal life."* (Mark 10:29–30)

CLOTHES

Gayness affects the wardrobe. There are clothes that say, "I'm gay" or "I'm gay and ready" or "Wouldn't it be fun?" Clothes convey messages. This most clearly happens in the case of transvestites and leathermen, but it is also generally true for anyone who has been in the gay scene for any length of time. It is even more so for men than women, especially the young, more feminine men. Clothes are important for people who are cruising. Thousands of dollars are put into obtaining a complete gay wardrobe and retaining such will have to be carefully considered. It is not good for a person to continue to wear seductive clothes that communicate gayness and attract potential pickups. Also,

clothes say something to the person wearing them, such as remind-
ing the person of old lovers and/or tricks. Some articles of clothing
may be retained but worn differently. Of course, it is not right to begin
wearing clothes that are heterosexually seductive. A Scripture to
apply here is 1 Thessalonians 5:22, *"Abstain from every form of evil."*

PLACES

The gay bar is, for many homosexuals, the center of an exciting social
life. Large metropolitan areas such as San Francisco, London, and
Mexico City have such vast homosexual populations that a person
may rarely have to step out of that community into the straight world
in order to conduct his/her business. Here in the Bay Area, gay men
who desire to turn away from homosexuality have had to move out
of the Castro and Polk Street areas. Likewise, gay women have had to
disassociate themselves from gay friends and lovers. If the "fire" is not
put out altogether, it is likely to smolder and smoke for a long while.
It may even start up again. The little black book being kept as insur-
ance against the whole thing not working out, communication with
ex-lovers when it can't be handled, magazines "for the article," old love
letters to fan the flames of the past, wishful ideas of the gay life being
good, negative attitudes against the heterosexual population, and so
on. These are not easily walked away from and tend to be causes for
stumbling. It is helpful to embrace the words of an ancient prophecy:
*"Remember not the former things, nor consider the things of old. Behold
I am doing a new thing; do you not perceive it?"* (Isaiah 43:18,19a).

FRIENDS

Everyone needs close friends, people to intimately relate to on an
honest basis. No one can make it without friends. This is true for gay
people as well as for heterosexuals.

Persons committed to the gay life are offended and threatened
when one of their numbers leaves the life style behind. It challenges
their own sexual identity and makes them wonder if they are right
after all. In some cases, gay people are happy to see friends "escape"
gayness, if it is obvious the whole thing was not working. In my experience, friends who have panicked by a person's exodus from the gay
community may prove to be a source of trouble to the one leaving. This
is true in other circumstances as well. In fact, it is a characteristic so

common to mankind that the Apostle Peter wrote of these "friends": *"They are surprised that you do not now join them in the same wild profligacy, and they abuse you"*(1 Peter 4:4). The false security of sin may be maintained so long as no one rocks the boat. When a friend leaves the gay life for Christ, that is earthshaking to the others. The tendency is to mock, criticize, and otherwise seek to bring the friend back into the fold where everyone can sink a little bit deeper. It requires great courage to walk away from sin and sin's companions.

> *Blessed is the man who walks not in the counsel of the wicked,*
> *nor stands in the way of sinners, nor sits in the seat of scoffers;*
> *but his delight is in the law of the Lord, and on his law he medi-*
> *tates day and night.*   Psalm 1:1–2

ATTITUDES

Gay sophistication is powerful and very subtle. Lifestyle pride is not taught explicitly nor spoken of openly in the gay community in general. It is learned by osmosis. "Gay pride," the public demonstrations of gay people intended to boast gayness, is the most blatant form of this sophistication. Perhaps it is a defense against overwhelming fears of the straight society; perhaps it is a justification for rejecting the heterosexual lifestyle. It may simply be more of the basic pride of man which is the organic sin expression. Whatever it is or however it works, it is there and must be vigorously dealt with by anyone hoping to live a heterosexual life.

"Homosexuality is better," "gay people are more sensitive and understanding," "gay sex is superior"—these and a complex myriad of other attitudes may serve as a glue connecting a person to homosexuality. It may be described as a "we/they" mentality and produces a deadly pseudo-sophistication that is difficult to overcome.

It is essential to rethink and reject much of the anti-straight propaganda. Ungodly, prideful attitudes about gayness must be put aside. A person committed to Jesus Christ finds his/her identity and value in that relationship with Him.

Some ex-gays may have a rough time getting along in a local church because of their gay oriented manner of life and negative way of thinking of heterosexuals. This may be more of a concern to some than others. Gay superiority must be discarded before the humility and simplicity of Jesus begins to be evident in one's life.

PORNOGRAPHY, MASTURBATION, AND FANTASIES

Magazines "for the article" are best left for the garbage man. Subscriptions to *Vector, The Advocate, Lesbian Tide, Blueboy, After Dark, Ms.,* etc., might be cancelled. Some have gotten into trouble by retaining porn materials even though they said they were just trying to "keep up on the scene." This requires an honest evaluation of how strong a person thinks he/she is, keeping in mind that we usually overrate our strength.

Generally, porn is used for masturbation, whether it is in the form of pictures or stories. Fantasies are usually enough for masturbation to occur, but outside stimulation is often desired. Although masturbation is not necessarily sinful or harmful, it can be. The casual masturbator is one thing; the person addicted to it is another. It is vital to get one's head out of the gay world. If masturbation continually ushers a person back into gayness, it should be rejected as best as possible. Of course, I do not mean that one can then turn to "heterosexual" masturbation. The Christian should not be captive to sex in any form. A tough, hard stand is necessary in coping with lustful fantasy of any kind, gay or straight. We can learn to submit our minds to Christ and to be free of domination by the never-ending quest for sex, sex, sex. Fantasy may be the last refuge of gayness for many people. Although it may never be totally gone, a great deal of very useful and fruitful progress can be made. Every possible toehold than can be cut away from a person's life will mean that much more possible success in marriage.

One more thing here though: guilt over repeated failure can be damaging. It is not the worst thing in the world to have trouble refraining from masturbation. Few there be who are able to avoid the practice. If it is something that simply will not go away, be encouraged not to go into guilt and a sense you are a failure. Sex is powerful and it is unrealistic to expect immediate results.

FETISHES AND AFFECTATIONS

A fetish is an object of sexual stimulation that is not normally a sexual stimulant for the general population. Although the word "fetish" originally meant inanimate articles used to stimulate sexual desire, it has become synonymous with the term "partialism," which refers to the condition of becoming sexually aroused by various parts of the human body. For instance, some people may be attracted to feet or elbows, facial hair, noses, ears, articles of clothing, etc. this is true for gays as well as heterosexuals. Fetishes, unless they are overcome, can present serious problems in a heterosexual relationship.

A fetish is something that is acquired. Through some complex psychological twist, sexual arousal became focused on something other than the whole person of the sex partner. Perhaps anxiety produced by the guilt of sexual sin was alleviated by attention on an aspect of a person rather than the whole person being used or abused. The fixing of anxiety—if that is what it is—is handled to some degree by fetishes, but since it is abnormal and ultimately damaging, the fetish will deter genuine sexual expression and pleasure.

Fetishes may be extremely hard to break free of. This is also true of affectations, which are learned ways of behavior that express, communicate, even advertise gayness. Affectations become second nature, unconscious actions. It is usual for affectations to begin to fade away when gayness is rejected. However, some may never be entirely eliminated, and many will persist without outside help.

The struggles against fetishes and affectations are best worked on with the help of others. Friends can help if asked, especially with affectations. Fetishes, since people are more self-conscious about them, can probably be openly discussed with that one special person. The prospective husband or wife is the perfect one to collaborate with in dealing with fetishes, affectations, and masturbation. It takes courage and discipline, but the overcoming of these obstacles is worth the effort.

RESOURCES FOR CHANGE

Most change is accompanied with pain. For most people, change seems to be in the context of kicking and screaming. We are resistant to altering behavior and attitudes, and tend to avoid truth and reality. This is, I believe, how it is for most of us.

THE TRAUMA OF CHANGE

The Christian is not ignorant of the trauma and suffering that is a real part of the authentic Christian life. Of course, it is possible to live an easy life and flow with things that are convenient and expedient.

Dietrich Bonhoeffer called this "cheap grace." If it is grace at all, the life of lip service to God (but actually following one's own way) is really no more than taking advantage of God's mercy. But then we may be fooling ourselves and it may not even be cheap grace but simply deception of the most hellish nature.

A person coming out of a homosexual orientation will suffer even if he/she never makes a move toward heterosexuality. The reasons a person would even submit to such pain are threefold. One, for the sake of the kingdom of God, we yield to suffering. *"I consider that the sufferings of this present time are not worth comparing with the glory that is to be revealed to us"* (Romans 8:18). Paul experienced a great deal of suffering in his life because of Christ. But he looked ahead to the kingdom and believed he had made the right choice. Two, we accept suffering for the fullness of life. Jesus promised us abundant life (John 10:10). This quality of life is for those who see through the shallowness of life without the Spirit and are willing to pay the price of death to the old man for new life in Jesus. Three, we obey Christ because we love Him. He said, *"If you love me, you will keep my commandments"* (John 14:15). By faith and obedience to Scripture we hold that homosexual behavior is sin. Therefore, loving Jesus means turning from gayness, and that means there will be suffering.

God sustains us in our suffering, particularly when it is suffering for Him. He does not necessarily take the suffering away, but He does help us endure. He gives us His strength and courage to cope with the pressures. And this is not an unfruitful exercise. We can see suffering the way Paul did, *"we rejoice in our sufferings, knowing that suffering produces endurance, and endurance produces character, and character produces hope"* (Romans 5:3–4).

THE CHURCH

Next to the personal ministry of the Holy Spirit to the individual, the church is an important resource for change. In fact, the church is a crucial arena in which the Holy Spirit operates to effect growth and change.

Not all people are comfortable with their own sexuality and the presence of an ex-gay, or practicing gay person, may present difficulty. My experience has been that Christians, and they are not necessarily homophobic, who may be challenged by the idea of homosexuality, will get over it. Homophobia is a label used too often, and I have found it is really and usually simply a conviction that homosexual behavior is scripturally errant. There is nothing wrong with this, of course, but it can be taken as homophobic by some people.

A church is to function as a family, an extended family, and this is the environment where change takes place best. Adjustments, stretchings, and corrections occur as a normal way of living in a church fellowship where compassion and forgiveness are exercised.

Love is supporting. When temptations come and failures, severe depressions, and desperate drives are experienced, brothers and sisters can be there in the congregation to be comforters and sustainers.

The church is normal. All children are born into a family (at least initially) and the church is God's family for His children. My personal experience has shown me that people coming out of the gay life have greatly benefitted from being with other believers in the mainstream life of the church. Often it is a person's first sustained (and healthy) contact with the opposite sex. It is a neutral environment where people can get to know each other in a non-threatening atmosphere. It works toward the normalization of relationships.

On the other hand, some churches may be toxic or dangerous. In most every community there will be a church that will be a good fit. There are no perfect churches, and even in a church where the pastoral leadership is supportive, there will likely to be some people who are not very mature in Christ and may tend to be judgmental and lacking in sensitivity. My counsel is to not give up quickly in an attempt to find a church that is Christ-centered and biblically grounded.

REALITY EXPECTATIONS

Real growth is slow. I understand it takes twenty-five years to reach physical maturity. Attempts at speeding that process up would be dangerous. This is obviously true where physical growth is concerned, but it is as true when it comes to emotional and spiritual growth. And it is especially true in regard to a change in sexual identity.

I have seen several attempts at quick change. Sometimes to prove to others that the gay life is a thing of the past, a person rushes into a heterosexual relationship. In most every case this has proven to be dangerous or worse. Good mottos for ex-gays should be "easy does it" and "one day at a time." The best change is gradual. A new sexual identity cannot be rushed. It is not a matter of faith, either. I do not trust the dramatic conversions where a person is totally different in a flash. It can happen, but I have never personally seen it. Not a few of the members of Love In Action have slipped back into the gay life. It happens. But we provide opportunity to get back up and continue moving away from it all. This is what counts–the getting back up.

Learning a new sexuality is perhaps the most major kind of change imaginable. Moving from lust to love, from seeing people as objects to seeing them as individual persons, is a slow process. Anyone from a gay past hoping for heterosexuality must have a healthy reality expectation.

3

Building a Relationship

Societies that observe the ancient custom of arranged marriages succeed in reducing the normal anxiety associated with having to find a husband or wife. Parents pairing off their children take from them the problem, but also the opportunity, of building a relationship with a person of the opposite sex that could lead to marriage.

Judging especially from the history of Western civilizations, but other cultures as well, arranging marriages is only rarely used, and there is a general prejudice against it. Biblically, though we read about some arranged marriages in the Old Testament, it is clear that seeking a spouse is normative. There is no hint of arranged marriages being "Christian" in the New Testament. Most people want to learn to love another person freely. This means growing in the knowledge of another human, developing a caring and heart-felt desire for a special one who can freely love back.

Building a relationship with another person, however, is risky and potentially disastrous. A few former gays have expressed to me the wish (although I'm not sure how serious they were!) that marriages were arranged. This chapter will deal with the process of learning to love another person.

WHY BUILD A RELATIONSHIP?

The kind of relationship referred to here can only happen when two people freely choose to be committed to and involved with each other. It means making a decision to work out problems and overcome disagreements. It means growing together bit by bit, persevering in love when it appears separation is possible. True love is built slowly and carefully; the instantaneous "falling in love" experience is a myth.

Love at first sight is likely to be sensual and sexual, which is only a part of the overall experience and state of mature love.

A love relationship must be built; there is no other way for it to happen. It may begin intentionally or unintentionally. Many of the best relationships begin unconsciously. Generally, it happens in this sense through two people being near one another: at the office, the woman at the next desk, that nice person who works with you on the committee, or that person two rows up who is a regular congregant. It starts out by accident, and somewhere along the line, there is a change, and no one knows why or how. Once it is recognized, one can begin to consciously build the relationship.

Since human beings have been created to love and be loved, it is completely normal that they build relationships. Not all of these result in a marriage. But when a person knows he/she wants a life with another person where love can be totally expressed, building a relationship is necessary. Even when a relationship with a person of the opposite sex does not lead to marriage, it helps our personal growth to be able to relate in a healthy way to the other half of the population.

It is in the process of relating and being stretched that we learn more of ourselves and are pushed and pulled in maturing. It is exhilarating and pleasurable to be comfortable with a person of the opposite sex. Not all gay people have difficulty in building significant friendships with persons of the opposite sex, but many do. Surface relations are fairly easy to establish, but moving on from there can be complex. Those who have developed the capacity to intimately love their sexual opposite did not easily do so. Relationships must be built slowly, stone upon stone, beginning with a secure foundation (which is Christ), with strong walls (against sin) and with the help of carpenters who are reliable and knowledgeable (the church).

Why build a relationship? The answer is this: it is a prerequisite for growing and loving, for sharing life with another, for sharing mind and body with a special person as a true family. Sex is an important part of this. Sexuality under God is pure and free, enabling lust to be merged with or lost in love, and passion expressed without guilt. These are just a few of the reasons for risking the core of your being in seeking to build a relationship.

WHEN TO BEGIN BUILDING

A person from a gay background should not (and often cannot) move directly from gayness into a heterosexual relationship. There should be a transitional period where there is no pressure to be heterosexual, a time to be asexual and to concentrate on spirituality in general. The call of the gospel is not to heterosexuality, but to follow Jesus Christ. The relationship between the believer and his Lord is primary and must take precedence over all other relationships.

Boys and girls go through a "curiosity stage" in learning to relate to the opposite sex. An interest in the other gender begins about age ten, but no dating usually occurs until the fifteenth or sixteenth year. The intervening years comprise this "curiosity stage," during which boys and girls get to know each other in nonthreatening ways. There is no pressure at age twelve to date, to make love to the opposite sex, or to consider starting a family. It is a safe period of time when sexual interest grows and various episodes occur which add to each person's knowledge of the opposite sex. Appreciation for each other can grow in a way which is natural and innocent.

People from a gay background can settle into the curiosity state as a normal process. There is no rush, or set goal to meet. It is essential to let nature operate unhurriedly and gently over a period of time.

The curiosity stage may be short, but in most cases, it will be of some duration. In children, it covers a span of years, lasting from three to eight (or more) years. At this time in our life, we need to trust God that He is doing what is best for us. While in this stage, a person may despair that he/she will ever be sexual again. This may be true, and that possibility must be honestly faced. But to push oneself to be actively heterosexual before the time is right is to risk regression and further pain. Good counsel is to accept and be glad for the curiosity stage.

REASONS FOR NOT BEGINNING A RELATIONSHIP

Another way of getting at why it is good to begin getting to know another person is to examine reasons for not beginning a relationship. This is perhaps the major wrong reason for a person from a gay background to prove that the homosexual life is over. "See, I'm not gay," is no motive to be involved with another person. It won't work in the long run. The end may be worse than what was before. No one needs to prove he/she is normal sexually. The Christian finds his/her place in Christ. This relationship is more central than any sexual identity. It is wrong to be homosexually committed, but it is not sin to be simply, slowly (perhaps ever so slowly) moving to heterosexuality. Normality for the follower of Christ is not based on a successful sexual life.

Christian communities, will often, out of ignorance, place certain expectations on persons coming from a gay background. We do not have to fulfill people's or the church's expectations. It is not expected that you must rush into a relationship with a person of the opposite sex. Such a desire must rise out of a person's own inner conviction and sense of knowing when it is true.

Sex must not lead us around by the nose as though we were animals. It must be submitted to Christ and the commands of Scripture, or we will be damaged. *"By rejecting conscience, certain persons have made shipwreck of their faith . . ."* (1 Timothy 1:19). Sex is to be in the context of marriage. To hurry marriage so that we can be sexual again is to hazard too much. This tends to make the other person an object rather than a subject. An object is known and is acted upon (sin in human relations), whereas a subject is a person who knows and acts (wholeness). If we are led by a neurotic need to become attached to a person, the result will be a sick relationship and will not, in the long run, provide true love and fulfilling sexuality.

It is at this point that competent counsel is helpful. Often, we do not understand our own motives. If plans and ideas are discussed with people of wisdom and experience in the church, many hurts can be avoided.

HOW TO BEGIN

To me, there is one key principle that should guide beginning, and that is appreciation. Simply stated, find a person you appreciate. Appreciating means valuing justly, being grateful for, being sensitive to, being aware of, and forming a favorable critical estimate of another person that expands into a desire to get to know that person more deeply. This is the culture from which love grows best.

Appreciating requires observation, conversation, time, patience, and a willingness to put yourself in places and circumstances where there are other people. Here may be encountered the fears of rejection. However, no commitment is eminent, thus the anxiety may be lower than if a person puts himself/herself in a position of mate hunting. I am speaking of taking it slow, exposure to others in a non-threatening way, and simply being present. In my experience, the church and its activities are ideal incubators for appreciation to begin and relationships to develop. Appreciation is learning about someone, an indispensable agent for healthy love. As learning grows between persons, love is built. Love is mostly knowing. It is hard not to love someone when you get to know them. Love is knowing enough of a person to begin to care about them and their living. It is in this light that we can see that if sex enters the picture at an early point in the relationship, it brings too much knowledge, but knowledge that can bring shame and guilt rather than love. Sex ruins friendships. Sex is safe, perhaps safer, in the committed love of marriage. Carnal knowledge is powerful in its effect and can short-circuit the learning process rather than expand it. It is impossible to overstate the necessity of keeping sex in its proper place. The appreciating process is destroyed by its entrance.

Learning to appreciate is a low-pressure operation. It can take place over a long period of time. It is not commitment; it does not have the anxiety of a dating experience. It is a letting things happen at a pace where there is plenty of time for praying and clarifying. It is safe exploring. It is neither defensive for offensive. It is being present with others and getting know and be known. It is communication where no physical contact is expected or sought.

The process of appreciating allows God to bring people to you and you to people. It is not a quest on your part. Learning to appreciate is a natural process, a process an ex-gay can deal with even if he/she is just out of the gay life.

WHAT TO LOOK FOR IN ANOTHER PERSON

This section is not intended to be over and against the previous section; it is intended to compliment it. Knowing what qualities a person desires in another can help guide and inform appreciation. It is very possible to begin appreciating and become attached to a person who will not be good for growing out of gayness or establishing a healthy and happy marriage. Inspired appreciation is a decisive element in building a relationship.

From my point of view, the chief concern should be for the other person's relation to Jesus. Christ-centeredness in both husband and wife will make a considerable if not the critical difference in making a successful married life. It is entirely right to apply Paul's words in 2 Corinthians 6:14–15b, *"Do not be mismated with unbelievers...or what has a believer in common with an unbeliever?"*

The words of Scripture are clear. We ignore and disobey them to our own hurt. Submission to God is a wise decision for anyone. We must remember that God as Creator knows what is best for His children and therefore seeks our good. Obedience to our Lord is the highest form of love. And not every "believer" is spiritual; there are carnal Christians, too. Do not risk your future on a person who is weak in faith.

I wish to further comment on the spiritual theme here. Spiritual compatibility can be expanded to include aspects of loving such as the ability to commune together. To commune in prayer, praise, worship, silence, and work. It is a joyous and peaceful thing to be able to be together and not have to talk.

Respect for the personness of the other is really a spiritual factor. Mutual esteem counts in bed and when friends and family are gathered together.

Openness in communication, the strength to be transparent is indispensable for realness in marriage. Openness is having a clear conscience before another person. It is knowing there is sufficient love and forgiveness to hear anything.

And there are other considerations. It is important to look for compatibility in the following areas: physical, emotional, intellectual, and goals.

It is important to be physically attracted to a person, sexually, figure/build, etc. It is not necessarily spiritual to ignore this area. I believe a person that is a potential mate should be sexually exciting. That is okay, it is not sin. The sin is only in the actual experience of lust or fornication. Appreciating another's body can be godly. You cannot fake sexual excitement, it either is there or it is not. Of course, it can grow when it is not there or not strong at first. Do not pretend though. It no one arouses you, settle back into the curiosity stage and be content with how far the Holy spirit has already brought you.

Emotional compatibility is important too. There needs to be a meeting of life force, libidinal energy. I am not trying to be esoteric here, but two people are radically different in temperament will have severe struggles in adjusting their lives together. Perhaps this is a bit obscure, but there are those who will understand as it suddenly fits their situation.

Then there is the intellect. Marrying across class lines is accep0table and right. Love does make a difference, yet it can present some very real trouble. Thinking together for two people committed to each other is a pleasurable event. Conflicts in ideas and knowledge are frustrating and potentially schismatic. Some share background in information, viewpoints, exposure, and experience make for a better fit.

Goals shared add meaning and purpose in life and this point can hardly be stressed enough. It ties in with not being mismated with unbelievers, but actually goes beyond it. Two people heading in different directions in their desires for living is simply going to produce problems that may prevent a real oneness. Particularly critical is where one person wants to be involved in ministry and the other does not. This may be too great a barrier. Sound thinking, courageous thinking is demanded at this point. Love covers a multitude of sins, yes, but divergent goals for living the few years Goad has given us on the planet is potential tragedy.

We look for someone we can share deep things, hard things, even grossly unpleasant things. We look for someone who can contribute to our identity, who seeks to be upbuilding and sup0portive, someone who works to help establish a sense of self worth. We look for someone who gives and is able to receive erotic love, brotherly, sisterly love, and God (agape) love. This is high minded stuff indeed but is there waiting through suffering over time.

SOME POSSIBLE BEGINNINGS

Tradition in Western civilization generally says that men initiate, at least overtly, the early forms of the relationship. Women have many beautiful ways of doing this as well. And let me say to women, most men are fearful of asking a woman out on a date. It poses the threat of rejection, and men usually will not risk much on a person they feel may turn them down. The quiet or shy girl unintentionally communicates she is standoffish. A girl in our church, who was not particularly attractive and had not much of a figure or charm, nevertheless had men swarming around her.

She had a way of making guys feel accepted. She talked and fussed around them. The phone was ringing off the hook. Strangely enough, a strikingly beautiful girl is often ignored by men. We all have inferiority complexes to some degree and feel like the gorgeous people will turn us down. At least that is how I felt many times. Datability is important. Please, ladies, I am not suggesting flirtatiousness, merely friendliness and openness expressed by a genuine concern for and interest in another person.

There are many young people in our church. On occasion, I am asked by girls why no one is asking them out. Not that I am all-wise about these matters, but usually it is clear to me why the problem exists. The girl is communicating that she is likely to say no, is uninterested in men, or is too spiritually above it all. In the girl's heart, she wants attention from guys and is anxious to date. Smiles, conversation, and warmth are what I encourage people to do in this situation.

For the guys, I usually say you just have to risk it. There is really no other way. My counsel is, take courage; after al, the female is a person quite like you are, with fear and anxiety over possible rejection. Make the call, strike up the conversation, be friendly, simply put the question out there. Do not leave it up to her to decide the nature of the whereabouts or kind of date; be specific. Lay out your plan for the date, but be flexible as to another idea or arrangement.

Simple inexpensive dates are best. Avoid elaborate arrangements, and keep it simple. A picnic, a ride on the ferry, a long walk, some TV watching, a cup of coffee at a local café—a few ideas. If you start big, it is difficult to keep that up.

Avoid trying to impress. Eventually, the truth will come out. Be yourself but be polite and courteous. Be honest about yourself, and do not create false impressions. Love comes from knowing the real person. There is no way I can explain it all here. It will require trial and error. There will likely be hurt and disappointment, also. One date may be it, and either you or the other person will have to make it clear. It is better to end an obvious mismatch earlier rather than later.

Space dating out. Once or twice a week is fine for early on. Immature people often overdo it. In some cases, there is a great romance for about one week, then poof, it is all over. Little by little is the principle. It takes time to know and be known. Being in different situations such as going on a walk, working together on projects, being in prayer groups, visiting friends, attending a sporting event, and so on, provide time to simply be together and help create normalness in relationships, making faking it nearly impossible.

Establish a bond through trust and honesty. Get the relationship off to a good start without wearing a mask.

Avoid finding fault or scheming to rearrange a person. Acceptance of another person is absolutely necessary.

A date should not be an encounter session, either. A person you date is not a counselee or a participant in a Synanon game. Treat a date with respect at all times. Put into practice what the Bible says about love as found in 1 Corinthians 13:4–7:

> *Love is patient and kind; love is not jealous or boastful; it is not arrogant or rude. Love does not insist on its own way; it is not irritable or resentful; it does not rejoice at wrong, but rejoices in the right. Love bears all things, believes all things, hopes all things, endures all things.*

CONTINUING A RELATIONSHIP

Continuing a relationship is basically growth in appreciation. There are so many intricate facets to every person, that a lifetime is required to absorb them all. It is best to love a long time. Like any solid structure, love is built slowly and carefully.

Relationships can be quite fragile in the early stages. Every step should be brought to the Lord in prayer. It is not as though one were walking on eggshells, but there are some definite pitfalls to avoid.

There are five essential elements to keep a relationship growing in a healthy manner. The first of these is forgiveness. Forgiveness is an everyday operation. The more intense a relationship becomes, the more forgiveness will be needed. It is impossible not to offend or say or do something wrong. A marriage requires "from the bottom of the heart" forgiveness. If two people are intimately living life and are being honest, there will be multiple occasions for forgiveness to be extended and received. Mark it down please: forgiveness is the core to any relationship. As Christians, people who have been forgiven much, we find it easier to forgive others. Our example is Jesus, who forgave those, and that is all of us, who were responsible for His going to the cross.

Secondly, unconditional acceptance is of huge importance. This is a part of love as is forgiveness, and it means loving without the neurotic or sinful need to change the other person. "I love you as you are" and not, "I love you, but..." A passage of Scripture that I love reflects this unconditional acceptance in a most beautiful way. It reads, *"Welcome one another, therefore, as Christ has welcomed you, for the glory of God"* (Romans 15:7). Jesus welcomes us as we are, sinners, poor, dumb, and blind. This is an example for us in how to love others. Rarely do we have opportunity to put this into practice in very much of a deep way, but in a relationship where love is growing, godly type welcoming and acceptance can be lived out.

Thirdly, communication, as everyone knows, is highly important. Getting that done is the challenge. If dating is always activity oriented, healthy communicating may not develop. Two people must sit and talk with each other about personal matters. It is not enough to discuss issues, movies, other people, and so on. Good communication depends on honesty in terms of feelings, likes, and dislikes. You have to sit down and talk with each other, listen to each other, and reflect on the content of the conversations. It is not easily done, or maybe it is better to say, rarely done. Yet, the deepening of a relationship depends upon this. This is something that takes time, so there is no sense in rushing it.

Fourthly, it is important to have a vision of the Kingdom of God, to have something in the center of a relationship that is bigger than the relationship itself. Two people mutually serving Christ bring a dimension into living the married life that goes beyond dining out at fine restaurants, attending concerts, and roller coaster rides. It brings purpose and meaning into the process of living. Living for Christ adds immensely to a relationship.

Fifthly, living with the peace of God at your core takes the edge off the relationship. God's peace and forgiveness is a fruit or by-product of serving Jesus and is given by the Holy Spirit of God to a person who has put Him first in their life. Two people who sincerely desire Jesus to be in the center of their relationship will experience the peace of God. This peace creates an atmosphere of freedom and helps displace anxiety.

Growing in appreciation month by month is the goal. Notice it is month by month. It takes months, indeed, years. Days and weeks are not enough. Such maturing will always be somehow, or somewhat, incomplete. Being in a marriage relationship is not a race that is being run. However flawed it may be—and it will not be wonderfully perfect at all times or maybe even reach such a state—it is yet the intention of our Creator as we see in the first several chapters of Genesis.

WHAT CAUSES RELATIONSHIPS TO FAIL?

This subject is so very broad that only generalizations can even be hinted at. If a person seeks perfection in another person, the relationship will last only until the flaws begin to appear. That may take only a few dates, or a few months, or a few years. No one is without flaws, even large faults. We are all sinners living a world fraught with that which is evil. Maturity calls for right evaluations and realistic thinking.

Treating a person as an object will destroy a relationship. We are subject, not object; we are not tools for the personal gratification of other people or to be used for personal gain. On the one hand, dating can degenerate into a means for satisfying sexual needs. Sex (fornication) ruins relationships. On the other hand, using another person for constant approval and emotional support will only result in the establishing of a neurotic dependency. Too often, there is pride of ownership, showing off a person like one would a new car. This is demeaning at best and a sure way to destroy a relationship. We do not ever own another person.

We must treat one another as children of God, people who have a heavenly Father who watches over them. We must treat one another as brothers and sisters, members of the Body of Christ. We must treat one another with respect, honoring, even exalting one another. A line from a song I remember from my childhood goes, "We belong to a mutual admiration society, my baby and me." It is an absolutely beautiful way of expressing the kindredness of two people.

HOW TO KNOW IF YOU ARE IN LOVE

This is a multi-faceted puzzle. When I am confined to a brief answer over the phone or otherwise hurried situation, I respond, "Would you want someone else to spend the rest of their lives with him/her, or do you want to be with him/her from now on?" The question is designed to get at the inner core of emotion and bypass the fears and neurotic entanglements. It is a "love" question, and if a person looks deep for the answer, it can go a long way in determining what the heart and mind are saying.

Love is not simply an emotion, but it is emotional all the same. Love is not simply romantic, but it can be romantic. Love is commitment, a longing to be with, to have and hold for the duration. Love is a desire to give oneself to someone else and receive in the same way. In its highest form, love is the concern to develop the maximum potential of the other person and have them experience the fullness of life.

People may fall in love with love. In our church, there will sometimes be a rash of marriages and engagements. They can come in spurts. Some of these people have fallen in love with love and need the attention usually given to couples on their way to getting married. Disaster can overtake these people, sadly.

Falling in love is a highly questionable thing, It is probably a myth. Usually falling in love turns out to be infatuation or an unleashing of the sex drive. It is often short-lived and very confusing. There are a lot of engagement rings rattling around in jewelry boxes, and broken hearts hurting because of the infatuation state of falling in love.

It is my thesis that love is built, as appreciation and concern grows month by month. Genuine mature love develops without the band playing or the bells ringing. It is almost imperceptible; it is natural; it is a process. It is the clear desire to "keep him/her to yourself as long as you both shall live."

Though it may be impossible to ever concretely know if love is happening, there are some indicators that love is growing:

1. There will not be a desire to date other people; there will be a desire to "get it in writing." Other relationships will seem unimportant and will begin to fade away.

2. A faith and trust will develop for that person, a confidence that you are safe with him/her.

3. That person will inspire you to be at your best in dress, conduct, and speech. A bit of a personal transforming along practical lines will occur.

4. A concern to be with and meet that person's family and other significant people in his/her life will arise. You will have a desire to get along with them or at least understand them.

5. There will be a growing caring about the practical details of that person's life circumstances, a concern that he/she is safe, healthy, and happy.

6. A pride in that person's accomplishments will develop, a sort of delight in his/her abilities.

7. There will be respect for the person you love. If there is embarrassment involved and fears that people close to you will find out, something is wrong, very wrong.

8. Being apart from that special person will cause you to feel lonely, and you will day dream and fantasize about with him/her. It will be difficult to wait for the times you can be together again.

9. Genuine love produces a desire to sacrifice for him/her, an actual looking for opportunities to give with no thought of return. The joy of giving is present in a love that is reality oriented.

10. There will be a desire to have family, to set up house with him/her. You will feel happy about any children the two of you may have.

11. When something happens to the one you love, you will identify with it, whether it is good or bad. When he/she hurts, so will you. And, you will want to act as a protector, and you will want to be there to help and support.

12. Love will be more than sexual, but it will also be sexual. Sex is a part of the love relation, but the desire for sex will be kept in proper biblical bounds out of respect. When you intend to marry a person, and genuine love is present, you can wait for the sexual aspect of the relationship to emerge at the proper time.

13. Friends and family around you will see the love. They will see and approve and rejoice with you. Beware when everyone is against the relationship. It is best to counsel with mature Christians at such a point. Do not be fearful of exposing your love to others, especially the spiritual leaders of your church family.

14. Real love, psychologically healthy love, is not so all consuming that you end up as a complete basket case. A balanced love relationship actually frees you to act sensibly in the world and does not confuse and distort your living. It will inspire and motivate, encourage and delight you.

THE PROFANING OF SEX

The Puritans were the sexiest people around, back in those centuries following the Reformation that began in the sixteenth century. The reason behind this is they had so previously repressed and controlled sex that it came squirting out at the edges wildly when the shackles came off. Repression is not successful, but the libertine excesses are worse in terms of realizing the fullness of sexuality. The provocatively clothed person is often more stimulating than nudity. I am speaking of the profaning of sex. When the hidden or apocalyptic element of sex is removed, sex becomes mundane, boring, and commonplace.

Sexual expression retained, sexual love held for marriage, helps bring about greater sexual joy than if it were treated as a trifling matter. And guilt, loss of respect, and embarrassment due to sin do not have an opportunity of intruding themselves into a beautiful relationship.

Observe the commands of God on sex, and yes, it will bless you. You, with the help of the Holy Spirit, in bringing your sex drive under control, will be doing yourself and the one you love a very great favor. Sex can wait; it is best when it is alive in purity, powerful and joyous, free and lovely. Sex touched with disobedience is not even close to what it could be.

Jesus said, *"Where two or three are gathered in my name, there am I in the midst of them* (Matthew 18:20). That can apply to the relationship of a man and a woman. Jesus being present with you makes who you are and what you do a divine event. Am I going to far on this, spiritualizing sex? I think not.

ENGAGEMENT

Engagement is the first concrete expression of love in terms of intentions to marry. Though it is a preliminary step, it is nonetheless important. Actually, it may have greater significance than the marrying itself. Engagement is something that should be taken very seriously, both for what it means to the engaged couple and to the friends and family. Therefore, engagement must not be rushed into, it must be soberly considered.

For the person from a gay background, engagement presents some potential problems. Sometimes, parents and significant others are not aware of a person's previous involvement in homosexuality.

If they are, so much the better. Being able to be open in this matter is extremely freeing.

If no one knows about your gay past, perhaps it is just as well. At this point in your life, it may be wise to reveal it, but this question must obviously be carefully considered. Outside counsel from the church or a marriage counselor could be helpful. It may be that the past should never be brought up. If the past is securely in the past, then it may be better to leave it that way.

The tricky question is, Should the parents of the person you love know about your gay past? Perhaps, the less that remains hidden the better. Openness and honesty is greatly facilitated when there is little or nothing to hide. If there is a real possibility of unsuspecting parents finding out or "seeing" it, then frankness may be called for. With homosexuality being so much more talked of and understood in our culture now than ever before, there is less risk of outrage and rejection.

Speaking for myself, this is an issue that I am unsure about, and one of the reasons for this is that each circumstance can be very different, so different that I have found myself unsure of the right way to advise. This calls for much prayer and solid spiritual counsel.

Engagement requires courage. It is a monumental stage for possible rejection upon the part of the person who does the proposing. It is best for the decision to engage to marry, and then to announce it, to be mutually decided upon. In most situations, this will naturally emerge when real love is present.

Engagement need not be a formal affair with rings and announcements. It may be by mutual consent and acknowledgement. It may be a state of relationship recognized as simply and purely as any truth is recognized.

"Keep it simple" is an art that can be practiced diligently at engagement time. Avoid wild displays and grandiose demonstrations. Letting it be, letting it happen is what you want. Letting others do the spreading of the word for you might be a good way to proceed.

Engagements can be long or short. A rule of thumb is, if two people have known each other for a long period of time (maybe two years plus), and family, friends, and fellow Christians approve of the relationship, a short engagement of three months or so is fine. However, if the relationship is short termed and few are aware of the relationship, a long engagement period may be called for, maybe even a year.

MARRIAGE PLANS

Marriage plans can be simple or complex. The bride is usually the one who has the honor and/or responsibility for the basic plans, though there is nothing in stone on this. Usually a couple will share in establishing the steps leading to the actual marriage ceremony. The actual size and extras of the wedding should be determined by the couple, realistically considering the expenses.

Weddings can be done very inexpensively. Often, guests are asked to bring dishes for a potluck reception, and the ceremony is held outdoors at a local park. If the couple are part of a church, this may be of great value and help. A large, elaborate, expensive wedding and reception are not necessary. But these are minor details in the overall picture.

When I perform a wedding, I ask the couple to come in for counseling. My approach is a simple one, and my outline follows below. The procedure on the first of two visits is to give them a list of practical concerns that I ask the couple to thoroughly discuss on the second visit. I let it be known there are no right or wrong answers. My concern is to make sure that the subject of each question has been looked at. The second visit consists of going over the list given on the first visit to see if there are any areas I could help with. If it appears there is more work to do, additional appointments are scheduled. Generally, I ask the couple to read one of the standard books on Christian Marriage. There are many such available, and these can be found where Christian books are sold. This process requires approximately two months, but three are better.

HERE IS THE LIST I USE:

1. If you want a family, how many children do you want?

2. When do you want to begin a family? (This question brings up the question of birth control, which should be contemplated early on.)

3. Do either of you intend to consider further education?

4. What kind of employment do you see for yourselves?

5. Who will keep the books? How will you set up bank accounts?

6. How will you make decisions on spending money?

7. How will you relate to your in-laws?

8. Where will you be living?

9. What faults does the other have? (This is calculated to see how reality oriented they are versus romantic views.)

10. How do you fight? (Here I look for violence and a person who clams up and withdraws, the latter being as dangerous as the former.)

11. What does it mean to submit to each other?

12. What will be your relationship with Christ and the church?

13. What will you do if problems are encountered in your marriage?

14. What does it mean to be in love?

The questions are designed to help overcome as many potential problems as possible. There will always be problems; there is no way that any marriage will be perfectly harmonious. There are adjustments to be made, problems to be solved, and there will be disagreements. It is just the way it is even for the strongest and well adjusted Christian.

THE HONEYMOON

Most people think of the wedding night and the sexual experiences when considering the honeymoon. And that wedding can seem extremely awesome, even problematic, to a person with a gay background. This is only to be expected and not feared.

Sex is one of the many ways of affirming love. It is not an experience to feel ashamed about. It can be an adventure of discovery with the person you love.

It is best to set aside the rigid role concepts, that is, putting down the ideas of what it means to be manly or womanly. The macho and feminist roles are culturally produced, to a large part, and not God ordained. People can develop some rather strange quirks that may reappear in a marriage. Some couples I have known, where one or both had a homosexual identity prior, went through some rather dramatic, even traumatic experiences on their honeymoon. What else would be expected? But those I have known who have carefully moved into their marriage and have been willing and able to talk about hot points, I mean, the embarrassing ones, have done well.

Sexually, one does not have to be an acrobat or super experienced lover. Indeed, the innocence of two virgins on their wedding night can provide for the loveliest possible sexual experiences. If you don't know a thing about what to do, admit it, talk about it, and go on from there. Both bride and bridegroom need to work at taking the pressure off the honeymoon.

A healthy attitude toward sex is essential. As best as possible, any negative attitudes toward sex need to be discarded. Sex is not sinful, shameful, or disgusting. Sex is a God given gift. God made sex, made men and women capable of it, and put into their hearts and minds the normal desire to experience it. Sex in marriage is lovely and honorable, sweet and pure. In fact, we are even commanded to engage in it. See Genesis 1:28 and 1 Corinthians 7:2–5.

Honeymoons are luxuries, in a way; no one has to have one, either. Often couples do not go away at all, but stay home and begin their married life without disrupting their lives.

Not everyone has sex right away, even on the first wedding night. (Let me tell you I have heard all kinds of rather funny stories.) Often weeks, and in some cases, months pass before full sexual relations are engaged in. This calls for maturity. Sometimes there are major sexual barriers that must be broken down, and they will be after some point in time. On occasion, I have counseled that a couple be affectionate, cuddle, engage in self and mutual masturbation, but feel free to not press for intercourse or oral sex. Let it grow; there is no rush, and this pressure is taken off the honeymoon.

Now some counsel learned the hard way: never go camping, and do not visit relatives. Be alone on the honeymoon, if you decide to have one. Stay in motels and hotels, eat out, do not travel too far away from home. Return home whenever you want to. Do not mortgage a home, empty a savings account, or take out a loan for a honeymoon. Do what is reasonable and natural. A honeymoon is just a tiny part of a big whole.

Theodore Isaac Rubin, M.D,. writing the column, "Psychiatrist's Notebook" for the *Ladies Home Journal*, May 1979, addresses the question, "How to Have a Happy Honeymoon." He gives ten points on how to have one. (Most of the points address first the wife.)

1. New husbands and wives should choose whatever kind of honeymoon they like! (a mutual decision.)

2. Remember that honeymoons can be stressful times and try to lessen the strain. (Talk about the fears.)

3. Feel free to postpone your honeymoon. (Honeymoons can come at any point.)

4. Let your own sexuality—and your husband's—unfold freely. (Take the pressure off sex.)

5. Beware of this thought: "If he loved me, he'd know what I wanted without my telling him. Telling spoils it." (Communication is central.)

6. If something dreadful occurs, don't think the marriage is doomed to a succession of similar disasters. (Growth is standard.)

7. Don't let popular custom run you out of town. (You do not have to go on a honeymoon at all.)

8. Don't use your bridal suite as an arena to test your own, or your husband's ability to love. (Sexual technique and expertise will develop.)

9. Keep your expectations within bounds. (Honeymoons can be boring and not as wonderful as often anticipated.)

10. Don't blame your husband for the anxiety you're almost sure to feel. (And don't let him blame you for his.)

When a Relationship Ends

Nothing hurts worse than a broken heart, and there seems to be no remedy but time and deliberate work at recovery. Nearly everyone experiences the pain of a relationship ending at one time or another. It is akin to the grief reaction that all humans experience when a loved one dies. It makes little difference who ended the relationship. There is a great sense of loss, confusion, shock, bewilderment, anger, and tears without end. However, as one song says, "It is better to have loved and lost, than never to have loved at all." One comforting thought is that millions before have been through it, have survived, and have gone on to love again.

What is the best way to react to a broken relationship? Cry! Go ahead and cry and moan—it's natural. Get it out, be mad and hurt, talk to others about it, rage at God if necessary. Those feelings are there, and we recover more quickly if we vent them. Repression or faking it merely puts it off, and when the emotion does come out, it may be in a destructive way. Write out your pain, express it in words, perhaps with a song or a poem to capture it. Release it without embarrassment.

Do not let a broken relationship pull you back into the gay life for comfort, or to spite the other person. A trip to the baths or the bar is no solution and will only increase the pain. This time, that hurt will also be accompanied by guilt. Avoid such irresponsibility; this is a time for real growth, not regression.

Pray for the other person you have been involved with. Turn the ache into a petition to God on their behalf. That person is a child of God and needs love and support. Though there may be no hope of resurrecting the relationship, pray that God will bless that person who has gone away. They are also human and may be suffering more than you. A source of immense hurt may be the thought of this special person making love to, and having a family with, someone else. When real love is there, this is usually a problem. Hope for God's best for them and a full life. Resentment is devastating; it will only hurt you. If you feel good about punishing yourself, get to a counselor immediately. This is the time to put 1 Corinthians 13 into action: *love is kind, not jealous, not resentful, it bears all things and endures all things.* Now is the time for a steady flow of faith in Christ. Perhaps it hurts so much, because the person you loved was more important to you than Christ Himself. When our priorities are out of perspective, there will inevitably be a reckoning. Let the ending of a relationship be the time to draw closer to Jesus. Let Him be the lover that never will go away. Nothing shall ever separate us from His love (Romans 8:35–39).

Avoid blaming yourself for the breakup. Often, it takes a while to discover that two people are not right for each other. Whether you were left against your will or you were the one who made the hard decision to end it, do not put the blame on yourself so that you feel that you will not try again.

Avoid the "rebound" reaction. Rebound often occurs when a person has been told that a relationship is over. The experience of rejection hurts so bad that people may run to another person, ignorantly rushing into another relationship without a thorough healing from the first one. Rebound situations do not work, because they spring from hurt, resentment, and all manner of ungodly attitudes. Wait on God; settle back. You have nothing to prove to anyone.

If a relationship ends, this does not mean God is saying to you that you will never be heterosexual. Life long heterosexuals also experience the loss of a loved one; it is a common experience of life. Why should you miss out on that experience which lies behind so many of our great songs, novels and poems? God has not singled you out, and the right person will come along.

Find a confidant, someone who knows you and will listen to you. Express your real feelings; confess the sinful attitudes you are struggling with. Get the dirt out; expose the hate and the fear by saying it out loud.

Try to accept any new relationship the other person has entered into. You may not be able to do this at first from the heart, but do it from your will, that part of you that makes decisions. Pray for him/her, pray for "their" happiness. This is a test of love and if you fail initially, do not give up.

Of course, you can praise the Lord. In not a few instances, when I have observed relationships end, I say, "Praise God." In my mind, I believe God brought deliverance from a dead end relationship. There can be blessings in disguise, and you will have learned things that can be applied to new relationships. Endings can make for wonderful beginnings.

4

Marriage and Sex

At first, this chapter was entitled, "Sex and Marriage". The word order was reversed to emphasize that sex is not the most important element of marriage. Sex should not be the prime reason for marriage, but in its proper place it is a blessing.

Above all else, marriage means commitment. It is a decision to live your life with one special person you love, to live your life fully with that one man or woman in front of God, man, and country.

There are many very real reasons people get married. Of course, one reason is because of love. This love demands commitment to that one person without whom life would seem unbearable. One measure of this love has to do with not being able to see that person you love being married to someone else. This is not jealousy, but a pure desire for that person to be fully yours.

People get married for intimacy, which is the desire to engage in mutual revelation of one's being to the other. Intimacy is being able to open up without fear of rejection, a free expression of the innermost thoughts and fears in a very safe environment. Intimacy is mutuality at its best. We search all our lives for a friend or lover we can truly be intimate with. Such love-fellowship can be found in marriage.

Companionship is another reason people marry. We have a need to share the experiences of life with others, and we may also have a fear of being that solitary person alone in this big and sometimes frightening world. Loneliness is one of the major scourges of life and many people in the gay life face it day in and day out. Loneliness is impossible to escape completely. In fact, I believe some loneliness is healthy, as it helps us evaluate ourselves and our relationships. But loneliness can also be a grave disease, even a killer. Marriage should provide an answer to loneliness, although you can be married and still be lonely. If your marriage is not a good one, it will not be a solution to anything, including the need for sex. However, good marriages centered in Christ can be an incredible blessing.

Another reason people marry is to have children. It is not wholly uncommon for gay men and gay women to team up in various ways to have children. Gay men have been known to pay gay women to have children for them. There is a major biological and psychological drive to reproduce, to leave behind to future generations your name and a bit of your person and life. Marriage is the legitimate arena for genealogy, and to have and raise one's own kids is a powerful desire in the hearts of both men and women. One of the consequences most often experienced by gays committed to life-long homosexuality is childlessness. Of children, the Psalmist writes:

Lo, sons are a heritage from the Lord, the fruit of the womb a reward. Like arrows in the hand of a warrior are the sons of one's youth. Happy is the man who has his quiver full of them! He shall not be put to shame when he speaks with his enemies in the gate. (Psalm 127:3–5)

A THEOLOGY OF SEXUALITY

It is appropriate to speak of a "theology" of sexuality because God made sex. His commandment to be "fruitful and multiply" (Genesis 1:28) is clear evidence for God being responsible for sexuality. The command (notice in the context of the passage it is a command) to "be fruitful and multiply" was given prior to the fall of man. Sex existed before sin entered the world, not after. Eve was given to Adam for far more than someone to talk to. It is obvious they must have been sexually attracted to and aroused by one another. Tim and Beverly LaHaye write, "Although we have no written report for proof, it is reasonable to conclude that Adam and Eve made love before sin entered the garden (see Genesis 2:25)."[1]

God designed the human body for sex. He designed it for reproduction and pleasure. The fact that He created our genitals for pleasure is

---

1   Tim and Beverly LaHay, *The Act of Marriage* (Grand Rapids, Michigan: Zondervan Publishing House, 1976) , p. 11.

very clear when you consider the massive number of nerve endings in the head of the penis and in the clitoris. The sex drive is not perverse or "dirty". The sex drive can be misused just as the drive for food may be misused, but that does not mean sex is not good and pure. We humans in general have perverted sex in so many ways that it is difficult, if not totally impossible, to experience the beauty of sex as it was originally intended.

Guilt has been securely attached to sex for too many of us. Part of the guilt is justified in that guilt naturally results from breaking God's laws. When a great deal of guilt has been experienced through the years of sexual sinning, it is hard to suddenly begin to think of sex as good, clean, and pure. But that is what sex is in marriage. However, sex is associated with guilt for many gays. Now, with marriage, sex scan be wonderful.

MAXIMUM SEX

It is necessary to distinguish between biblical or Christian sexuality from the sexuality of the "world". There is a big difference. Society in general has no sexual standards at all. It is more a question of what a person can get away with. Most non-Christians probably feel the Christian view of sex is too narrow or restrictive. In my view, the opposite is true. The Bible has much to say on how sex is used, on the personal nature of sex and its delicate and fragile quality. The Bible does not degrade sex in any sense. It speaks against indiscriminate sexuality because sex is to be with persons, now with objects. The Bible casts down the idolatry of sex and lifts up the beauty and dignity it has when used properly.

Sex requires freedom. When sex is experienced under a cloud of secrecy, guilt and sin, this becomes a bondage that warps it. Freedom and a clear conscience before God and humans are essential before sex can be the experience it should be. Many people have "had" sex, but have never experienced the fullness of sex in the context of exuberant love. Animals have sex, but we are more than animals.

Our freedom in Christ should enhance our sexuality. There is not guilt or sin, but only the joy of God-given physical loving. Those whose sexuality is stimulated by a touch of evil will have to adjust to the rightness of sex. I have known many people who could be sexy in the bushes or in a tearoom, but not in the marriage bed. This sort of perverse orientation is the result of years, perhaps decades, of living a double life. Perhaps beginning in early life, when faced with parental disapproval of things sexual, sexuality is driven underground. As the intensity of the sex drive grows with advancing years, the connection is made that what is unacceptable conduct is the most desirable and exciting way to go. Unfortunately, this is the result of wrong parental attitudes toward sex and is passed from generation to generation, destroying any possibility of knowing sex as God intended it. Sex may become secretive, hidden, and distorted. Some gay people have come from counseling because, for them, pleasure can only be achieved when sex is engaged in outside of their marriage. Without that sense of the forbidden, the evil, and the perverse, sex has little meaning or excitement.

The grace of God helps us deepen our relationships and establish them on solid footing. Christ working in us can begin to develop trust and security and give a desire to love in terms of giving to another person. Jesus said, *"It is more blessed to give than to receive"* (Acts 20:35).

We give to persons, not objects. Christ helps us see every man or woman as a person and convicts us when we treat them as objects. Most sexuality outside of marriage is this kind of usury, a sexual act conducted between people making objects out of each other. Maximum sex is possible only in a love relationship that submits to the law of God.

THREE TYPES OF LOVE

Eros is the category of love with which sex is usually connected. However, eros love is broader and actually includes a passion for anything, even music and art. Eros love is good, but it can be perverted. It is a love created by God and is essential for good sexuality.

Phileo love is brotherly love, a relating to persons as kin and developing with them honest friendships. A wife or husband can be and should be loved with phileo love.

Agape love is God's love, the relating to another person solely for their own good. Agape loving is seeking the very best of all that God has for them in Christ. This is the highest form of love there is. It is the love with which God loves us and asks us to practice toward others.

Agape love is essential to the marriage relationship. Without it, no marriage can be all it could be. It is a love God must infuse into people's lives; it is a love that cannot be grasped with human hands. Agape love is a gift we me must ask the Giver for.

There are false loves, which are the counterfeits of eros, phileo, and agape. Paul, in Colossians 3:5, writes: *"Put to death therefore what is earthly in you: immorality, impurity, passion, evil desire and covetousness, which is idolatry."* "Immorality" in the Greek New Testament is "porneian" which means fornication, the term used to express all sexual relations outside of marriage. "Impurity" is any sexual looseness, including fornication, adultery, homosexuality and premarital sex. "Passion" is simply lust, which involves mental sex or sex in the head which captivates a person and leads to continual unclean thoughts. "Evil desire" is not necessarily sexually oriented, but is a lusting for the world that is opposed to God, a lust for the mythical or the temporary as opposed to a seeking for the ultimate reality, God Himself. "Covetousness" is the desiring of that which belongs to another, whether that be a wife/husband, car, house, etc.

These false loves are the common fare of the people who seek their own carnal desires. They cannot be the foundation of anything permanent. They will prevent or distort any real sexuality from developing, sadly enough.

THE MARRIAGE BED UNDEFILED

Hebrews 13:4 is an important verse in regard to marriage. *"Let marriage be held in honor among all, and let the marriage bed be undefiled; for God will judge the immoral and adulterous."*

The context of the passage shows that the writer of Hebrews warns against basic sexual sin, which can disrupt marriages. But on a broader basis, we see the godliness of marital relations. I believe that whatever kind of sex occurs in the marriage bed is honorable. However, no one should force any form of sex. If a wife is set against anal sex, for instance, out of love a husband should not force her to submit. Every sexual form must be desired by both husband and wife. It is the love expressed that is crucial. The Bible tells men to "take" wives honorably and not in a lustful manner. The selecting of a wife/husband is to be done in the context of righteousness, not lustfulness. Sexuality in the Bible is free and earthy (natural), not binding or perverse. Sexuality is most sexy in this context.

The Body

The drawings of the male and female genitals found at the end of this chapter are perhaps not necessary, but there may be people who are not aware of the basics. As I studied the charts myself, I found I was ignorant of many things. For a man, it is important to know the location of the female genitals and the positioning of the various orifices. It is necessary to know where and what the clitoris is. I had been married at least ten years before I knew myself. No one, not even my wife, ever told me. However, I know now and am making up for lost time!

Women tend to be more aware of the fundamentals than men, and for many reasons. The male organ, though complex, functions rather simply and its basic operation is rather obvious.

If there are any unanswered questions on the basic physiology of the body, I recommend any sizeable bookstore or library. If you have the courage, you will find there are many helpful books available today. It is better to consult a serious work rather than *Playboy* or *Playgirl*. It is important to be informed as to the functioning of the genital systems and how they are best stimulated. I highly recommend a college textbook, *McCary's Human Sexuality* by James L. McCary and published by D. Van Nostrand Company. It has everything anyone ever needs to know.

All bodies are beautiful, fat and thin ones, big and small ones. Every body is created by God for pleasure and, with some exceptions, is able to carry out the sexual feats necessary. Bodies are funny. Few people have picture-perfect bodies. Nudie magazines often find it hard to get subjects. Every body has "flaws" and imperfections. There are pretty places and not-so-pretty places on every body. But we don't love bodies; we love persons. A body is only one aspect of a person.

In the gay life, the body is overemphasized. Youth and physique are at a premium. It often reaches exaggerated proportions and may be the cause of a great deal of rejection. There may need to be some significant adjustments made in the mind of many people from gay backgrounds regarding physical beauty. Old concepts of what is desirable and exciting may have to be rejected. We must become less body conscious and much less youth oriented. My mother used to say, "beauty is only skin deep", which is true enough.

Agape love means unconditional acceptance and that must be broad enough to include the body. Acceptance of the body means acceptance of fat, big breasts, small breasts, big penis, little penis, droopy buttocks, wrinkles, scars, blemishes, and other assorted little funny things about bodies. Loving is accepting. It may require some real work and reorientation. Do you imagine God loves us more if our bodies meet up to the silly social ideas of what makes for a "sexy body"? I do not mean to be overly simplistic, but uncritical acceptance of what our culture says about beauty is to accept a lie about the body. All bodies are beautiful.

Bodies need exercise. To a major degree, we cannot change how we look, but we can be in shape. Toned muscles, sensitive reflexes, clean blood system, etc. all help make for a fuller, more active life. My counsel is work to get in good physical shape. Jogging and skipping rope are excellent; you do not have to join a gym or a spa, although they are nice. It is easy to become neurotic about all this, especially if someone is pressing us to "look better". Avoid such pressure and only "work out" for yourself.

EROGENOUS ZONES

The whole body is erogenous. Of course, some areas are more sensitive than others. The most sensitive areas are the clitoris on the female and the penis (especially the head) on the male.

The genitals are therefore the most erogenous zones. In addition, there are the inner and outer thighs, the buttocks, and the abdomen. Knowing the location of erogenous zones is not as key as knowing how to touch or otherwise handle these zones. Nothing succeeds as much as learning to relate to the one you love with consideration, understanding. and easy gentleness.

There are non-genital erogenous zones too. These are the breast and nipples (on both male and female), the small of the back, the neck, and all orifices. The mouth and the anus are highly sensitive and can be sources of considerable sexual pleasure.

Sexual expression must be mutual in that both people desire it. No sex act should be forced. Anal sex is fine when both partners desire it. The same is true for oral sex. There is always a bit of lust in the sexual act, and this passion is acceptable and not sinful, I believe. Indeed, there is a legitimate sort of lust or passion that is going to be present. Perhaps we don't know what lust is, but that real sexy feeling that is experienced with the one you love is not sinful lust.

THE PSYCHOLOGY OF SEX

The mind and body work together. However, it seems that under normal circumstances, the psychology of sex is more essential to sexual pleasure than the physiology of sex. Even if the body is physically equipped and able, if the mind is filled with fear and anxiety, sex will either not happen, or it will be a painful and regrettable experience. To a great degree, the mind pushes the physical buttons. A woman can perform the sex act even when she would prefer not to, but a male cannot, since an erection is usually essential. A man who has difficulty obtaining or maintaining an erection may still engage in many sexual acts and please his mate.

It is said that men are more physical, more aggressive, and more demanding than women. This may be true to some degree. Perhaps this issue will never be adequately resolved. The question is whether this seeming tendency of men is a part of their basic makeup or whether it is culturally determined. I really do not know. It is not bad for a man to be aggressive and more physical, if he is gentle and considerate. Some women desire a man to "master" her and this is fine, but to have to submit to a man because he is stronger is not what a normal woman wants.

Women are said to be more psychologically oriented than men. By this, I mean they respond too much more than just the physical makeup of the man. Women are often more concerned with caresses and touching. A woman responds to a sense of security from her lover. Many women need to feel safe and protected, or to put it another way, to be covered by the man. The physical act of lying on the woman symbolizes the man's safeguarding the woman. The sense of well being is essential to a woman's full sexual expression.

Although these differences exist in the male and female, I believe there are far more similarities. Even their bodies are very much the same. The role differences are more distinguishing than the physical makeup. Men and women are one species; both are human beings. We have the same needs and hopes; we share the same fears. We are flesh, blood, and bone. The distance society has placed between men and women is artificial and mythical. Especially in gay life, this distance is often emphasized and exaggerated. In many cases, the opposite sex is put down and despised, and totally wrong attitudes are unconsciously adopted. Man is male and female. (Genesis 1:27). When Adam saw

Eve for the first time, he said, *"This at last is bone of my bones and flesh of my flesh; she shall be called Woman, because she was taken out of man"* (Genesis 2:23).

Preparing for marriage does not require an extensive analysis of the male/female psychology. It is, in most instances, enough to follow the words of Jesus when He said, *"So whatever you wish that men would do to you, do so to them"* (Matthew 7:12). Perhaps it had never occurred to us that this "golden rule" could be applied to love but, of course, it must be. Self-centeredness in sex will surely destroy it. According to Paul, the *"wife does not rule over her own body, but the husband does; likewise the husband does not rule over his own body, but the wife does"* (1 Corinthians 7:4). Biblically then, sex is "other" oriented, a giving out. There is receiving, but it is pure receiving from someone who is intent on giving. The Creator's way is far superior to any device of the creature.

MEN AND SEX

Men seem to be more aggressive and more demanding in sex than women. At least, some men may be so characterized. This does not mean a man is going to be inconsiderate or brutish. A man can be an initiator and highly sexy, but still be gentle and soft.

Men, particularly men from a gay background, have felt that women are too slow in sex. They may be fearful that they may not get enough sex. This may be a fairly common concern. Some aspects of the male gay scene are highly sexual. There may be a dozen or so sex partners in a night, with that many (or more) orgasms. Obviously, there will have to be some major adjustments for men who have expected that sort of sex which is abnormal and not really sex at all. It has been my experience that sex in committed love is far more satisfying than meaningless orgasms. A loving woman can do a lot to change a man's mind and even help to change the sexual patterns. It may not happen overnight, but it can change.

TURN-ONS

There are some things that particularly excite men. I do not mean to be crude, but helpful when I say this. Every person is different, and some people may be repulsed at some of the turn-ons listed below. This list comes from a group of ex-gay males.

hair on body (some men dislike a smooth body)
smooth skin (some men dislike a hairy body)
smile (sweetness and approval)
firm holding versus a too gentle touching of genitals
good conversation (ease into sex)
challenge
tight buttocks
large, firm breasts (some men like small breasts, though)
pretty face
relaxed (little pressure)
modest dress, but slightly revealing
outgoing, warm personality
concern
private and romantic setting
clean (very critical for ex-gay men)
good smell
rubbing
good dancer
caressing
fondling
respect
mutual interests
affection and attention
touching
back rubs
sighs

This list could be many times longer, but enough is given to get the basic ideas across. All of these points will not turn on every man. In fact, some may turn them off. A woman will have to be a good detective to find the things her man likes.

TURN-OFFS

No one can avoid doing things that will be turn-offs, but with time, it is possible to avoid the obvious. A man knows that no woman is going to be a superwoman (if he doesn't, he may need to be told). These turn-offs are not tongue-in-cheek, and not every man is offended by the same things.

Passivity (some men like women who are initiators)
non-communication (a woman needs to tell a man what she likes)
digging fingernails into the back
teeth on penis
cigarette breath
hairy legs, underarm hair (but some men like it)
aggressiveness
fat
body odor
sloppy in dress
macho females
lead-ons
using sex for gain
excessive make-up
drunkenness
bad teeth
cursing
over talkativeness
know-it-all women

I will admit that some of the items on these two lists I barely understand.

MALE COMPLAINTS

This is a continuation of the "turn-offs", but are areas that require some comment.

Women talking during sex bothers some men. This is especially true of laughing or giggling during sex. Love talk is fine if it is not excessive. Cleanliness is of vital importance, and most ex-gay men desire a clean woman. They wonder how a woman can be really clean sometimes, since women menstruate, and the organ seems difficult to properly wash.

Women need to avoid comments like, "Oh, I see you have gained weight", or "I believe you have some new grey hair." Put-down comments should be forgotten entirely.

The worst possible question is, "How come your penis is soft?" If the man's penis is soft, either he is not ready or he is struggling with anxiety. Such a question may promptly end the event entirely, or, at the very least, greatly increase the anxiety. Anxiety causes adrenalin to flow and that effectively stops any erection.

Women need to avoid acting like a mother. Nothing could be worse for many gay men. Women should avoid being too passive or too aggressive. This may require some real ingenuity. If a woman is too aggressive, it can be threatening to a man. It communicates to him that he may fail or is failing. Being overly aggressive may cause a man to freeze. Passivity to the extreme puts all the pressure on the man and can therefore produce anxiety. A woman can gently explain what she likes and can lead a man into her. This last point is important. There have been many erection failures when there is repeated failure to enter the vagina. Many men desire a woman to be firm in holding their genitals, and some men desire almost a rough playfulness. A man should communicate what he desires or should be asked if necessary.

Many men enjoy sex more when it is obvious, by such clues as sighs and movement, that a woman is really liking it. It is not good to be inhibited in sex.

WOMEN AND SEX

Women from gay backgrounds, and perhaps most women, fear sexual demands from men. Women who have accepted and internalized the negative aspects of feminism about men will have considerable blocks and fears to overcome. The reverse is true for men who have lived in a strong gay community. The attitudes picked up are not natural but are sub-cultural. To me, the key element is seeing each person as a child of God, as someone for whom Christ died. We all have our problems and defenses against rejection. Gentle love is powerful in combating the evil effects of hate and prejudice. Women have generally been more sexually victimized than men and have some very legitimate fears regarding the sexuality of men. Nothing I say here is going to be a turning point for anyone, but the glory of change is worked out on a day-by-day basis.

TURN-ONS

There is no doubt I am on shaky ground in discussing these "turn-ons" and "turn-offs". I risk offending and misleading and, of course, it is all quite artificial and exceptional. However, there may be some helpful points buried in the upcoming lists.

> touching (not of sexually overt places on the body)
> kissing
> caressing
> nibbling
> stroking
> cleanliness
> hugging
> rough housing (for some women)
> back rubs
> honesty (good communication concerning likes and dislikes)
> love talk (romantic and/or sexual)
> body rubbing
> gifts (small tokens of appreciation)
> slowly undressing (as opposed to mad stripping)
> sighs of contentment
> respect (shown in gentle caring)
> long foreplay (very important)
> spontaneity
> sincerity
> taking time (not a rushed sexual encounter)
> humor
> being protected

Of course, each woman is different in her likes and dislikes. Good lovemaking takes time to learn. Satisfying sexual relationships can take years to develop. Patience, of all the fruits of the Holy Spirit, will have to be working or there will be continual frustration. Couples who have been married a long time, if they have worked at it, will have better sex lives than those married only a short time. There are no simple answers or programs—love is built slowly.

TURN-OFFS

> macho males (number one!)
> men who hide feelings
> short foreplay
> insistence (pushing for sex regardless of a woman's needs)

being treated as a sexual object
rowdiness
sloppy appearance
unclean
body odor
unshaven
poor manners
no privacy
being compared with others
possessiveness
no conversation
vulgar language
insincerity
selfishness
cruelty
messy hair
no cuddling after orgasm
being questioned about having a climax

FEMALE COMPLAINTS

This is a continuation of the "turn-offs" section, but these are areas that require some expanded comment.

Foreplay is more important for the woman than the man. Men have to learn to be slow and sexy. A man may tend to rush into oral sex or intercourse, but this can work against the woman. Caressing, gentle stroking of the body, etc. are very important. A woman's sexual response may be less physical than a man's. She requires love and consideration; she needs loving that takes time. Generally, the longer the sexual foreplay, the more likely it is that the woman will be satisfied sexually.

Premature ejaculation is a problem, since that usually ends the lovemaking and leaves the woman unsatisfied. For men who have this problem, there are ways to deal with it, ways that are actually quite fun. This will be discussed later in this chapter under dysfunctions.

Women fear that men will be too rough. Some roughness may be acceptable. If sadomasochism had been a part of the previous sexual orientation, it should not be carried over to married life. I am familiar with the "S and M" scene and have read Larry Townsend's, The

Leatherman's Handbook. Guilt is the primary dynamic in sadomasochism; either guilt is internalized (therefore, there is a need to be punished) or guild is vented outwardly (there is a need to inflict punishment). This complex psychological phenomenon becomes attached to sex to the point where there is not sexual satisfaction unless there is opportunity to deal with the guilt. Guilt is increased by the S and M sexual behavior and so the problem is continually compounded. If sadomasochism or some related form of it is present in the person's life, it should be dealt with directly. Good communication must go on between a couple, so that the right level of "roughness" is ascertained.

There needs to be a further word on sadomasochism here since a growing number of gay people and some straight people are experimenting with it. Sadomasochism is a frantic effort to find love, but it is a dead end street. It can have an iron grip on a person. It is such an enemy to the mind, body, and spirit that it must be attacked harshly through prayer and competent counsel. Sadomasochism is so far from the normality that to the person who practices it, the world of married heterosexuality will seem strange and unfulfilling. The pride that accompanies the S and M scene must be rejected. It is a case of calling good evil and evil good. In addition, the idea that S and M is true freedom to be who you really are must be viewed as a sick rationalization.

The guilt and condemnation that is so ineffectively subdued by the leatherman's pride and pseudo-sophistication must be washed away by the blood of Jesus Christ through repentance and faith. No less than a radical turning to Christ will suffice. It is a question of all or nothing. Galatians 2:20 must become a key verse for anyone heading out of the life of sex and pain: *"I have been crucified with Christ; it is no longer I who live, but Christ who lives in me; and the life I now live in the flesh I live by faith in the Son of God, who loved me and gave himself for me."*

A woman's clitoris is sensitive and should not be handled as roughly as the head of a man's penis can be. A man should massage around the clitoris and try to avoid direct rough contact with it, unless the woman requests otherwise.

Women often complain that men are unimaginative in sex or that they are inhibited in sex. Sex in lesbian life is usually far from unimaginative or in inhibited. This relates back to the discussion on foreplay. Gaining uninhibitedness takes time and depends on open and honest communication. Problems must be talked about, rather than being repressed. Satisfying sex cannot be learned in a rush. Much of it depends on respect, trust, and unconditional acceptance. Dull sex usually comes from an inhibitedness on the part of one or both people. The real roadblock to exciting sex is freedom from put-downs. This allows security to exist because of non-judgmental love. When these develop, sex opens up and flows. This may take considerable time and patient understanding, but the rewards are worth it.

BLOCKS TO SEXUAL AROUSAL

This section is included in order to touch on points that do not seem to fit elsewhere, since this subject has been discussed in various ways throughout this chapter.

A sense of disapproval will put a stop to lovemaking as quickly as ice water. Critical remarks about technique in the middle of making love will do damage for sure. Unflattering remarks about a person's body will do the same. Love means acceptance, putting the other person first and seeking to build them up. If a person's body style is offensive, it is best to realize that before anything serious develops.

There are fears that can devastate sexuality. One of these fears is anxiety over performance. When there have been many former lovers, gay or straight, there is always the fear of being compared. It is almost impossible not to compare. There are no simple answers, but a direct dealing with this and related fears may prove valuable. Identifying fears and being able to discuss them are the chief tools in overcoming them.

There is the fear of embarrassment. Concern over an erection, size of penis (women often prefer an average sized or even smaller penis, because it is easier on their bodies), body build, size of breasts, scars, hemorrhoids, body hair (excess of lack of) and many other body features can block sexual arousal.

Fear of pain, especially for a woman, can definitely block sexual arousal. A man should not act in such a way that a woman must bear pain in order to please. Even when a woman has vaginismus (a constriction of the muscles in the vagina which is often psychologically based), a man can still give and receive sexual satisfaction. Pinching, scratching, and biting are usually not appreciated and can block sexual arousal.

Privacy and freedom from interruption are important to sexual arousal. Time must be set aside for sex, quality time when all else is suspended. It must especially have priority over business. Equally important is that love making it is to have priority over the demands and expectations of family members, friends, and in-law relatives. We too often relegate the things of God to the bottom of the list, placing the demands of those around us to that immediate priority position. We should not capitulate to the clamor of the world. If God thinks sex is important, then we must believe that it is important enough to provide time and space for it.

All roadblocks to sexual arousal may not be easy to eliminate. Again and again is the need for honest and open communication. Perfection is not going to happen; do not expect it, rather be reality oriented. Life has a way of backfiring on us, especially when we try so carefully to put the pieces together just right. Being able to talk and laugh at our mistakes is precious medicine.

POSITIONS OF LOVEMAKING

Considering the number of books available today that depict various positions for lovemaking, I did not feel these needed to be included here. A trip to your local bookstore will easily give you all you need.

Positions are basically easy to learn. With a little imagination, most people can come up with a dozen or so positions for intercourse and/or oral sex. Experimenting is fun and is better than following directions in a book. James L. McCary's book, *McCary's Human Sexuality,* covers the basic positions very sensibly and has adequate explanation for each one. Also, Tim and Beverly LaHay's, The Act of Marriage, carries information on positions of lovemaking.

Probably the best position for lovemaking is the "missionary position" with the man lying on top of the woman. This position allows for maximum pleasure. There can be intercourse, kissing, fondling, and kissing/sucking of the breasts, stimulation or massaging of the clitoris by the man or woman, manipulation of the testicles and/or penis by the woman, possible stimulation of the anus, and wrap-around hugging. Also, it is the position that most clearly expresses the man's "protecting" the woman. This position is comfortable to assume and allows for wide variation. But anything that two people agree on and like is acceptable.

Far more important than any position is the love that is communicated between two people. It is the mutual commitment that makes for maximum sexual pleasure.

Sexual procedure can begin simply with: (1) being together, (2) conversation and communication, (3) privacy and security, (4) hugging, touching, and caressing, (5) kissing, (6) fondling, (7) massage of erogenous zones, (8) oral sex, (9) intercourse, (10) hugging, caressing, kissing, (11) affirmation of love. Some of the steps from (6) to (8) may be left out and the process may, of course, be varied, but this 11-step concept incorporates the essentials. Probably, the key steps are 1,2,3,4,5,6,10, and 11. Many couples enjoy no more than this and are satisfied. An orgasm is not a requirement.

It is best to relax about positions. As they are needed, they can be discovered. Some sexual ignorance need not always be a problem. In fact, it can be an avenue to a lot of fun.

STAGES OF SEXUAL RESPONSE

Climax occurs toward the end of the sexual act. There is much that precedes it. The sexual act is a kind of process that can be broken down (artificially, of course) into four stages.

The first stage is arousal or excitement. This occurs differently for men and women, and these differences have been previously discussed. Physically, the penis of the male is enlarged as it becomes engorged with blood. The clitoris of the female is also engorged with blood, as are the minor labia of the genitals while the major labia are spread flat. The body is getting ready for intercourse and the person knows it and wants it.

The second stage is a plateau. The vaginal opening enlarges (expanding from one to three inches in diameter), the clitoris shrinks, and the woman is ready to be penetrated. The penis is ready and performs penetration and continued thrusting into the vagina. In the male, the climax reaches a point of inevitability at this point, but not so in the female. This is a stage of prolonged pleasure, baring a premature ejaculation.

The third stage is orgasm. The physiology of it for the male and female is complex; it is not completely understood. It is unnecessary to discuss it here. The climax of orgasm or "coming" is an intensification, usually for both partners. It is, of course, not necessary to reach orgasm for there to be sexual pleasure.

The fourth stage is resolution. The man is generally tired and finished after his climax, at least for some minutes. But for a woman, this is not necessarily so. A woman may have multiple orgasms. But though the man may be feeling exhausted and the penis loses its erection, the woman may not be satisfied. The man can help her receive continued pleasure by massaging her clitoris. This is to help ensure that the resolution is not a disappointment. The orgasm, especially for a woman, is secondary to intrinsic security and a sense of committed love. A man must realize this, and not simply turn over and go to sleep.

WHAT THE SEX ACT CONFIRMS

Sex for human beings is more than a biological act. What it communicates and confirms is highly complex and is perhaps beyond words. Although I am limited, there are still a few observations that I want to make concerning the sex act and what it is saying.

Admiration for the sex partner is intensely expressed in the sex act. Admiration is an element of love; it is marveling esteem mingled with pleasure and delight. Making love to a husband or wife is joyfully recognizing and affirming the other person's worth. It is a way of praising the one you love. It is saying that the other person is the one you value more highly than anyone else, the one person you hold up in esteem to the point that you engage in very intimate sexuality with him or her.

Desire is confirmed through the sex act. This is the passion that makes sexuality alive and exciting. It is a wonderful sensation to have another person concretely let you know you are intensely desirable. It helps overcome any sense of inferiority about one's body or loveliness. To be desired is upbuilding and promotes the concern to please the other person. It is wonderful to know you arouse passion and sexual excitement in the person you are most concerned about.

Appreciation is expressed in the sex act. Sex is not a reward mechanism, although it can be a way of saying "thank you." Appreciation is a returning of love; it is loving because of being loved. It is not self-centered or exploitive. Committing oneself sexually to the one you love is to confirm the fact that you appreciate that person.

Normalcy is confirmed in the sex act. Married love is right with God, and the sex act attests to the legitimacy of a person's sexuality.

There is a peacefulness that may be experienced in sexuality that comes from the knowledge that your personal sexuality is approved and acceptable. For the ex-gay, this sense of normalcy should not be underrated. It is the one of the many rewarding changes God makes in a life. It is a feeling of equality with the world, as self esteem suddenly rises, and a peace and contentment replaces long held feelings of inadequacy. To one who has never considered themselves normal, marital sex brings a joyful happy glow of self-assurance. There should be no guilt in the love expressed between a husband and wife. If there is, it can be overcome. There is no shame or perversion in the loving of a man and woman committed together in marriage.

DYSFUNCTIONS

Dysfunction means that a normal process is not working properly. Here we are concerned with sexual processes. Many people experience one or another form of sexual dysfunction. In recent years, there has been a proliferation of sex therapists, professionals trained to deal specifically with problems related to sex. Though these experts have been somewhat maligned and have been the butt of many jokes, they perform an important service, and their research has contributed significantly to the successful treatment of sexual disorders.

In some instances, sexual dysfunction is the result of some physical disorder such as birth defects, diseases that affect the muscle coordination, diabetes, etc. However, most sexual disorders are psychological in nature. McCary says, "The condition underlying most instances of sexual failure or malfunction is fear."[2]

Poor sexual experiences from the past contribute to sexual problems. Though sex therapists may not deal with the question of "sin," I believe using sex outside of marriage where lust and selfishness reign, results in fear and anxiety. We have already seen that God designed sex and has said it is good. The negative does not come from God, but proceeds from us doing things our own way.

McCary says that "religious orthodoxy is responsible for a significant degree of sexual dysfunction."[3] The brand of religion does not

---

2   James L. McCary, *McCary's Human Sexuality* (new York: D. Van Nostrand Company, 1978), p. 297.
3   ibid.

matter; it may be any of the major world religions. "Men and women with sexual difficulties are almost invariably the victims of negative sexual conditioning during their formative years."[4] Religion is a tool people can use to authenticate their neuroses and weird ways. Christianity should produce balanced people in regard to sexuality and would do so if the Bible's teaching on sex were correctly communicated. When a person has grown up with negative attitudes about sex, therapy is aimed at building a good view of sex in the person and overcoming wrong attitudes about the body and sexual pleasure.

THE FORMS OF SEXUAL DYSFUNCTION

There are six forms of sexual dysfunction, three in men and three in women.

SEXUAL DYSFUNCTIONS IN MEN

For the male, there are: (1) erectile dysfunction, or impotence, (2) premature ejaculation and (3) retarded ejaculation.

Erectile dysfunction is the inability to obtain or maintain an erection of the penis. This is a common problem and one which men fear.

There is much misunderstanding about impotence. Many men will awake in the morning with an erection, give it no special thought, then find they cannot achieve erection when the time for intercourse is at hand. The source of this circumstance, its psychological nature, will many times be overlooked and the man will think he has a physical problem. While an erection may be necessary for a man to reach climax, it certainly is no such handicap for the wife. Men tend to view the situation as a loss of manhood. It becomes intensely embarrassing and causes an over-reaction that only deepens the problem. The cure lies mainly in the hands of a caring, loving wife who will not allow her husband to suffer humiliation but will come to his aid through reassuring words and actions. Frequently, the man will have a semi-erection which, while too soft for penetration, is still engorged enough to achieve orgasm through manipulation from the wife, either orally or digitally.

It is well for the wife to keep in mind the five pleasant messages that are may be conveyed to an impotent husband. One is verbal;

4   ibid., pp. 297–298.

that is, words of reassurance, words of love and worth. The other four are non-verbal and are as follows: sight, touch, scent, and sound. How these are communicated is a test of the wife's innovative qualities. The key message must be that the husband has not failed, lost his manhood, or is still gay. It is very damaging when a husband equates impotency with the "once gay, always gay" mindset.

It is necessary to understand that a man will achieve an erection when there is sufficient stimulation by the woman and when his anxiety level is reduced.

For men from gay backgrounds, impotence at first is an expected experience. While there may be some who escape this problem, most do not. It is important that in pre-marriage counseling, this subject is discussed so that the anxiety level may be diminished.

It is advisable for ex-gays to adhere to the principles of sensate focus, outlined briefly in this book and detailed in other publications. This should begin right from the start of marriage. Sexual behavior is clearly learned behavior and the adjustment from a same-sex partner to an opposite-sex partner is definitely possible. The wise path to follow is to enter marriage without pressure and expectations that cannot be met. If there is fear and repulsion at the thought of intimate relations with the opposite sex, this should all come out and be dealt with in counseling prior to marriage. The ex-gay at the time of marriage enters into a commitment to the spouse and that commitment means that they are willing to begin a re-learning process that will bring sexual happiness to both individuals. The husband who avoids all sexual contact with his wife because of impotency is clearly violating Biblical principles and is defrauding his wife.

In secular psychology, it has been found that the use of fantasies may be of some value. The Christian must weigh this carefully in the light of Matthew 5:28. The method used is to allow the ex-gay husband to use homosexual fantasies in foreplay with his wife, then at the time of orgasm to switch to heterosexual focusing, especially on the wife.

When impotency comes about in a long-standing marriage, the causes, while somewhat obvious, are nevertheless baffling when panic sets in and rational thinking becomes impossible. The key reasons for impotency in this situation are: monotony, career in top priority, fatigue, excessive food intake, aging fears, and an attraction to someone else. Of course, we have not mentioned that there can be physical problems, but the chance of this is proportionally small. However, while considering the physical related problems, a significant cause may be reactions to drugs, either medially administered or otherwise. There seems also to be a combination of the physical and the psychological in that the body has two systems at work. One system, the parasympathetic, controls sleep, digestion, and erection as well as many other things. The opposite system, the sympathetic, prepares us for emergency situations as well as other things. If interrupted during sex, the sympathetic system releases adrenalin which effectively collapses an erection.

Premature ejaculation is a problem in that it usually prevents a woman from completing her orgasm or enjoying sex at all. Many gay men learn to reach climax quickly, sometimes in less than thirty seconds. This is especially true for men who have been used to tearooms, "glory holes," the bath, and other quick encounters. In fact, some men have learned to reach orgasm quickly without even obtaining an erection at all. If this has been a characteristic of gay sex, then premature ejaculation may be a troublesome factor.

There are many methods of dealing with premature ejaculation. Currently, the method that seems the most effective is a form of sensate focus that educates the husband to the triggers that lead up to the inevitability of ejaculation. It is recommended that one read *Intended for Pleasure* by Ed and Gaye Wheat, Revell Publishing, where the procedure is detailed in Chapter 6, "The Tortoise and the Hare." Among the traditional cure procedures, the following are worth noting. The stop/start method is simply reaching the point of orgasm and withdrawing stimulation. After several denials of orgasm, the man is then allowed to release. Another method would have the man masturbate earlier in the day before sex is intended, or to allow the man to climax in some fashion before intercourse is to take place. Multiple condoms will desensitize the effects of intercourse enough to prevent premature ejaculation, but is generally not a method that is well liked. The use of a lubricant may be a cause, and although a small amount might be necessary, curtailing excessive use may help at times. Nupercainal is a long-time prescription, but its use must be watched carefully as it can bring discomfort to the woman. Of course, there are many psychological reasons involved. A man insensitive to his wife's needs may never know a problem exists. Some men gain pleasure from using a woman and take delight in forcing her to meet his needs only. This would be a rare instance in the case of an ex-gay man.

Retarded ejaculation is the failure to ejaculate even when there has been adequate stimulation. This problem is less frequent than the other two forms of dysfunction. However, even if this is rare, it is still relevant to the issue of marriage for the ex-gay. This condition is a counterpart to premature ejaculation and comes out of the same matrix. Some men in the gay lifestyle, particularly the bath and park scene, have discovered that when they climax, the interest is lost and for them, and the adventure is over. Through long-time conditioning, they have delayed orgasm to such an extent that they find themselves unable to achieve orgasm on a regular basis. This problem also should be thoroughly discussed in counseling before a marriage takes place. Treatment of this condition requires the involvement of a sympathetic wife who does not stress the problem but continues to show satisfaction with her mate. As the new circumstances become familiar and comfortable, the realization will come about that the methods of the old lifestyle are no longer needed. This may not be a conscious appraisal, but one that occurs subconsciously.

SEXUAL DYSFUNCTIONS IN WOMEN

The three forms of sexual dysfunction in women are: (1) sexual unresponsiveness, (2) orgasmic dysfunction, and (3) vaginismus. This section will not be as lengthy as that of sexual dysfunction in men since there is an overlapping of the two. Also, fewer explanatory comments are needed since they have been made in the section on the male.

Sexual unresponsiveness, or general sexual dysfunction, is similar to erectile dysfunction in the male. A woman receives little or no erotic pleasure from sexual contact. The basic physiological mechanisms are not triggered and vaginal vasocongestion and lubrication fail to occur. Also, the clitoris does not engorge with blood.

Orgasmic dysfunction occurs when a woman, even though she enjoys sexual contact and is normal otherwise, has difficulty reaching a climax.

Vaginismus involves the woman experiencing pain from intercourse sufficient to block sexual pleasure and consequently prevent orgasm. The muscles that surround the vaginal opening either have spasms or fail to expand when penetration is attempted, or there is pain felt within the vagina during the action of the penis going in and out. The fear of the pain of intercourse seems to keep the muscles from relaxing. In addition, penetration may be viewed as an unwelcome invasion.

SENSATE FOCUS

The method of therapy for most sexual dysfunction that seems to be in common use and was developed by Masters and Johnson is called "sensate focusing." There is not space here to outline this seemingly fruitful form of therapy, but a brief account may be of value.

The aim of sensate focusing is to re-establish the positive, pleasurable sensations, and attitudes naturally present in early childhood. The central element of this therapy is the sense of touch. By the process of physically sensing the body through massage, feeling, caressing, and exploring all the various areas of the body with the hands and fingers, a new and positive response to the body and sexuality is established. Inhibitions and any sense of bodily embarrassment are dealt with as a couple learns of one another without actual sexual expression. Intercourse and other explicit sex are denied the couple at first. Fears and anxieties are dropped as the naturalness and beauty of sex comes to the fore.

There are three phases to the treatment. In Phase I, all genital stimulation is avoided. This is the phase of touching and feeling the body, which is meant to eliminate fears and bring a couple into intimacy without the dread of having to perform sexually. Orgasm in Phase I is not permitted. One at a time, the couple is instructed to stroke and touch their partner, but not to touch any explicit erogenous zones. The person doing the touching is to concentrate on the pleasure he/she is receiving from giving pleasure to the one being touched, and the one being touched on the pleasure he/she is receiving. This is to go on for several days and each session is to last about two hours with 25–30 minutes on each side per person. There is to be open communication about likes and dislikes and other pertinent information.

Phase II involves gentle and seductive stimulation of the genitals. The intent is to generate sexual arousal and again, as in Phase I, orgasm is to be avoided. The couple should discuss how they feel about genital and oral sex. Oral stimulation is not necessary for this process, but may be included if the people desire it. If one person is particularly opposed to oral sex, it is best left out until it is desired.

Each person attempts to sexually arouse the other—first one at a time, then simultaneously. There is to be no pressure or goal to obtain an erection. Intercourse is not permitted, but oral stimulation is allowed, if acceptable. Each person should communicate what they want and for how long, and when to move to other areas of the body. A woman especially must tell the man what is arousing to her, since he has no way of telling what works (the woman can observe an erect penis). The people must be careful not to over-stimulate and produce an orgasm. This phase is to be maintained for several days. If there are problems encountered at this stage, more counseling and therapy are necessary before preceding any further.

Phase III begins when there is a positive reaction to Phase II. This last phase is aimed at simply to produce orgasm through intercourse, mutual masturbation (using vibrators is acceptable), or oral sex.

Sensate focusing is a form of direct treatment for sexual dysfunction, although there are others used by sex therapists. Sex therapy should not be shunned when there is a need for it. Most sexual problems can be solved, and sex therapists have done much to help many thousands of couples

BASIC PRINCIPLES OF DIRECT TREATMENT

As previously mentioned, sensate focusing is a form of direct treatment of sexual dysfunction. Joseph LoPiccolo, in an article entitled, "Direct Treatment of Sexual Dysfunction" in the *Handbook of Sex Therapy*, describes seven principles of direct treatment of sexual dysfunction.[5]

1. MUTUAL RESPONSIBILITY

All sexual problems are shared; one person is not solely responsible. LoPiccolo writes, "The husband of an inorgasmic woman is partially responsible for creating or maintaining her dysfunction, and he is also a patient in need of help."[6] Both people are responsible for arriving at

---

5   Joseph LoPiccolo and Leslie LoPiccolo (eds.) *Handbook of Sex Therapy* (New York: Plenum Press, 1978), pp. 2–7.
6   ibid., p.3.

a solution to the problem. When both partners accept responsibility for the sexual dysfunction, one person does not carry all the anxiety, nor is he/she under pressure to be the one who changes. This is the first, and perhaps the most critical, of the seven principles.

2. INFORMATION AND EDUCATION

Many people who experience sexual problems are ignorant of the sexual process and techniques. Education on these points is not likely to prove successful in alleviating problems, but can at least set the stage for further treatment.

3. ATTITUDE CHANGES

All of us pick up negative attitudes toward sex and our bodies from society, parents, and religious institutions. These concepts will be detrimental to healthy sexuality. Sex therapy aims at improving attitudes towards sexuality. For example, letting women know it is acceptable to enjoy sex and express excitement (even wildly) is an example of attitude change. Often, people have problems with vaginal fluid and semen, imagining these natural body fluids to be "dirty." Essentially, these fluids are proteins and there is nothing unclean about them. Their presence indicates sexual arousal and pleasure. Rather than being repulsive, genital smells can be viewed as adding to the experience.

4. ELIMINATING PERFORMANCE ANXIETY

The general media presents people who are beautiful, highly sexed, and incredibly skilled at lovemaking. All this is quite intimidating to many people who feel they fall far short of that entirely unrealistic standard. Counseling can help people come down to earth about sex and beautiful bodies. It is difficult for anyone to be sexually successful when they feel they have so many inadequacies. Patients are taught to be not so intent on performing and achieving climaxes. A man who has trouble obtaining and erection is instructed to not engage in intercourse but to engage only in genital stimulation, as is the tactic in Phase II in sensate focusing.

There are many similar applications concerning sexual dysfunction, all designed to reduce anxiety. Letting each other know that it is fine to masturbate to achieve sexual satisfaction helps reduce anxiety about the need to perform.

5. INCREASING COMMUNICATION

Couples need to be able to express their likes and dislikes about sex. They need to honestly communicate their sexual needs. During sexual intercourse, a couple can be trained to give feedback on what brings pleasure. Sexual fantasies can be discussed, and special stimulants can be mutually evaluated. Good communication on sex can help a couple reduce fears and become more relaxed with each other.

6. CHANGING DESTRUCTIVE LIFESTYLES AND SEX ROLES.

Often, persons with sexual problems give sex a low priority in their lives, reserving sex for late at night when both people are tired. There are many innovations that a couple can make, such as mini-honey-moons, sex in the early evening, the afternoon, or the morning when kids are off to school. One-day trips to a motel can be highly stimulating. It is necessary that sex be considered important and not just something that happens when it happens.

Couples need to spend time together in shared responsibility, day-to-day activities, hobbies, and lots of good conversation. A chronic deterrent to good sex is the typical situation in which the husband is too tired to be a good lover when he comes home from work, but the wife is hoping for some meaningful interaction with him then. Solving this may require some real creativity. One way to deal with it is occasional afternoons off, the husband helping his wife with the after supper housework to free up time in the early evening, dinner out and an early return home, and many other possibilities. A husband and wife can work it out together for the sake of their marriage.

7. PRESCRIBING CHANGES IN BEHAVIOR

Prescribing changes in behavior is the basis of direct treatment and the basic methodology in sensate focusing or "pleasuring" exercise that have previously been discussed. The therapist directs the sexual behavior until the goals are reached.

REALITY

If a couple understands the concept of sensate focusing, it can be of much help, even without the aid of a therapist. The procedure depends largely on open and honest communication. In my mind, it is essential to be able to enjoy one another and not put a major emphasis on sexual performance. A relaxed attitude is basic and very helpful. Climaxes are nice, but not mandatory. Sex is not everything, and sex techniques can be learned easily enough. One couple I counseled was having no sex at all, but were in love and definitely happy. They began, under my suggestions, to lie naked side by side, masturbate themselves, and then talk about it. This lasted for months. The next step was masturbating each other followed by talking about it. Again, this lasted for months. They reported it was fun and that they'd had some good laughs over it. They used a vibrator for a while, and then began having intercourse. This occurred sporadically at first, then regularly. The entire process took well over a year. They developed insight into themselves, their fears, and their needs, and all the while their love for each other developed and matured. They successfully removed the pressure and inserted fun into their sexuality. Occasionally, we still look back and laugh together about the whole process.

Sex is not a science; lovers are not machines. Even with the best instruction, two people may not be able to do everything right. Sex is often bungled.

After reading this chapter, some people may think a jigsaw puzzle is easier figure out. Don't worry about all the subtleties and tricky concepts. Pay attention to some of the intricacies only if they apply or can be of some help; otherwise, relax and ignore them. A major requirement for a satisfying sex life is a good sense of humor. Sex will happen, one way or another. It is just a part of living; it is not the whole of life. God has made us capable of getting it done, and if we rely on Him, He will help in moving us into the gift of sexuality.

NOTE:
On the following pages are diagrams from the original thesis showing exterior and diagramatic views of male and female genitalia and internal sexual organs.

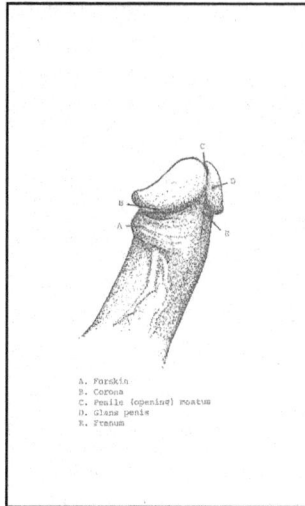

A. Foreskin
B. Corona
C. Penile (opening) meatus
D. Glans penis
E. Franum

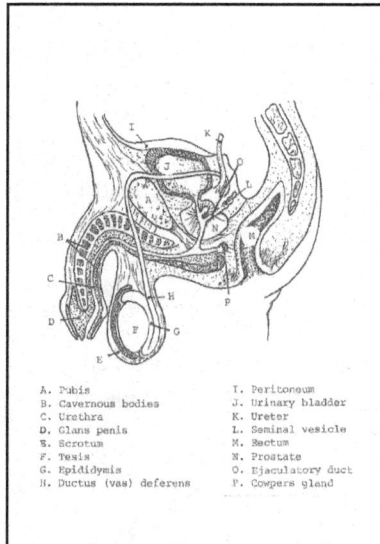

A. Pubis
B. Cavernous bodies
C. Urethra
D. Glans penis
E. Scrotum
F. Tesis
G. Epididymis
H. Ductus (vas) deferens
I. Peritoneum
J. Urinary bladder
K. Ureter
L. Seminal vesicle
M. Rectum
N. Prostate
O. Ejaculatory duct
P. Cowpers gland

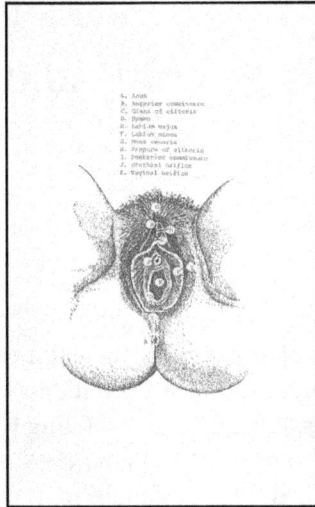

A. Anus
B. Anterior commissure
C. Glans of clitoris
D. Hymen
E. Labium majus
F. Labium minus
G. Mons veneris
H. Prepuce of clitoris
I. Posterior commissure
J. Urethral orifice
K. Vaginal orifice

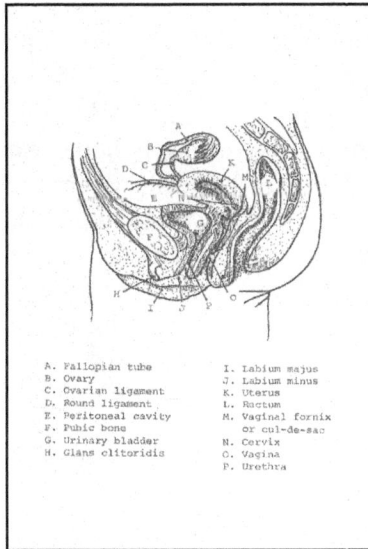

A. Fallopian tube   I. Labium majus
B. Ovary   J. Labium minus
C. Ovarian ligament   K. Uterus
D. Round ligament   L. Rectum
E. Peritoneal cavity   M. Vaginal fornix
F. Pubic bone   or cul-de-sac
G. Urinary bladder   N. Cervix
H. Glans clitoridis   O. Vagina
                           P. Urethra

5
Marriage Combinations

This manual is written for people who are coming out of a homosexual lifestyle. To consider marriage after years of being sexually attracted to persons of the same sex is a major change in orientation. To be as helpful as possible, a chapter dealing with specific marriage permutations and the special problems they suggest seemed very necessary. In other words, the gay male marrying a straight female, the gay male marrying a gay female and a straight male marrying a gay female are the marriage combinations. Each circumstance must be approached separately for maximum benefit, since each combination suggests varying problems.

The terms "gay" and "straight" are likely not the best of words that might be used. By "gay," is meant a person who is ex-gay, a person who has rejected homosexuality as his or her lifestyle, but whose sexual orientation has been nearly exclusively homosexual. By "straight," is meant a person who has been basically heterosexually oriented.

There will be considerable overlapping in the discussion of the three possible marriage situations. In two instances, we have the gay male and in two instances, we have the gay female. Often the same statements will reappear. I would rather have it that way than to miss important considerations.

Not apologetically, the material in this chapter is simply a beginning. It is short but could be much longer, if I had the ability to make it so. This is new ground for me, an area that never suggested itself prior to the onset of the writing of this manual. Perhaps more material will be forthcoming from people who read this. Any contributions will be appreciated.

My sources are: one, my own experience as a pastor to ex-gays;

two, a brain-storming session with members of the Love In Action ministry; and three, a thoughtful consideration of the many ideas that came forth. Biblical applications are made where possible. The word of Scripture is always our most reliable source, not only because the Creator knows best, but also because God's view assists us in transcending our own limited concepts. Our sophistications tend to obscure truth, especially regarding homosexuality, which is one of the great mysteries of life.

The material in this chapter is problem oriented, centering on fears and obstacles that may be present when, for example, a woman from a gay background is marrying a man who does not understand homosexuality. Of course, there will be couples who fit into one of the three categories, who nevertheless do not have to deal with many of the obvious problems outlined in each section. I may have missed them altogether, or they have resolved (or never had) the problem under discussion. There is always the possibility that I will stir up trouble where none existed before. Various people's circumstances are so different or specialized that, although a couple's category is explicitly described, the inner dynamics are of an entirely diverse nature. Such is the risk when homosexuality is the topic.

A married or soon-to-be-married couple should not be reluctant to seek professional help. Sex therapists perform a very significant work and should be relied upon when necessary. Sex therapists are not running massage parlors but are trained specialists in treating sexual dysfunction. I suggest consulting with your physician or minister in locating a qualified sex therapist.

GAY MAN—STRAIGHT WOMAN

I have observed that many heterosexual women are attracted to men with a gay background. Gay men often have developed manners and ways that are very pleasing to women. Too many non-gay men in our culture play the macho role, which is generally offensive to many women. Men from gay pasts have often rejected such dishonesty and are in touch with themselves to an extent that many men in the general population are not. I have seen ex-gay men make wonderful husbands to heterosexual women.

GENERAL PROBLEMS

A gay man may be repulsed by the smooth, hairless body of a woman. He may have a difficult time being sexually aroused by her, regardless of how beautiful she might be. Not all gay men share this fetish or partialism for hair, but many do. The sight and touch of hair on a man's body can be intrinsically tied to sexual arousal. The answer is not for a woman to begin hormone treatments! Honest discussion of the problem is an effective tool; patience and time will help. A process must evolve during which a man learns that hairlessness is good and can be sexually appealing. Sensate focusing may be applied in this particular case, even perfect for it. This is a learning problem, as an old pattern is unlearned and rejected when she finds out her body is not a big turn-on to her husband.

Other feminine characteristics may be stumbling blocks, too; for instance: long hair, breasts, larger or broader hips, shaved armpits, and even women's clothing styles such as bras, blouses, and dresses. These signs of femininity may have previously been sure fire triggers to repulsion and disgust. For many years, the mere sight of feminine things like nightgowns and sexy clothes may have produced feelings of disgust. These are not insurmountable barriers but are a definite trouble spot on which to work.

If a man has a strong hair fetish, it is fine for a woman to not shave. A woman from a gay background may not want to, anyway. This is not a concession but is an act of love.

The straight woman who plans to marry an ex-gay, if she loves the one to whom she is engaged, will want to make the marriage night as easy as possible. About two months before the marriage, she should have a physical checkup. At that time, if she is a virgin, her hymen should be checked to see if it is going to give any problems on the wedding night. Perhaps some experienced males might enjoy stretching the hymen on the wedding night, but it is best to alleviate this problem beforehand. At this time, she should also discuss with her physician what type of contraceptive to use. She will want to start pills prior to marriage or have a diaphragm or IUD designed. Also, if a virgin, she will not want to prolong the sex act for her own benefit. If the husband is able to achieve erection, it is best to allow him to climax quickly, and then bring his wife to climax through manual stimulation. This is because any prolonged sex will cause considerable soreness in the woman and an unwillingness to have intercourse again soon.

To the bride who is not a virgin, avoid the urge to compare with other sexual partners, mentally as well as vocally. While both the virgin and the experienced woman should guide the penis into the vagina, the experienced woman must carefully avoid the exhibition of too much knowledge in the sexual area, or her husband will feel intimidated.

Prior to marriage, time should be spent in exercising the P. C. (pubococcygeus) muscles. In American gay culture, perhaps somewhat over 50% of gay males have anal sex as their primary outlet. In other cultures, this runs to nearly 100%, possibly due to hygienic circumstances. What this means is that the gay person is used to the tightness of the sphincter muscle of the anus. Tightness is a quality highly regarded in gay circles and is used in gay terminology to describe something good. Women are thought of as loose. When gays have seduced a married man, they feel they have given him something far superior to sex with a woman. Often a married man coming for counseling will say, "When you've had the best (a man), how can you go back to your wife?" However, some have also said, "Once my wife began to exercise those P. C. muscles, things have never been so good." These muscles are not affected by exercise used for any other part of the body. They are not interconnected but are isolated and can be strengthened only by a specific method outlined in many marriage books. (See *Intended for Pleasure.*)

Something that a wife should realize is that a man's sexual urges continue during her menstrual time. So many women overlook this important fact, and one of the most frequent complaints we hear is that the wife has no consideration for her husband during this time. This will be a peak time of testing for the ex-gay husband and a wise wife will always make sure that her husband is sexually satisfied during this time when intercourse is discontinued. If there are any ripples in the marriage, this is the critical time when the husband has a ready excuse to return to gay activity. His rationalization might be, "My wife has rejected me" and he knows those who will welcome him and satisfy his needs. This one point might save a marriage and may be a most important element in this book.

FEARS

At the top of the list is the fear of the inability to perform sexually. Probably no other fear is as great as this, and it may persist for many years. It is here that a woman can do the very most for the man she loves, although there are no easy answers. Most importantly, a woman must take the pressure off and be sure to never berate her husband for failure to obtain an erection or for failure to reach orgasm.

Pre-marital counseling will want to include a discussion of this particular fear. Getting it out in the open is a first step in conquering fear. Heterosexual men often face this problem too; it is certainly not a phenomenon that exclusively troubles gays only.

There is a fear of not being understood by a heterosexual. Gay people find it hard to believe that a straight person could ever know what is really like to be in their shoes. No doubt they are right, but one does not have to understand to be sensitive, and to listen and to love. Understanding in terms of having "been there" is not a requirement for love to grow. A mature woman will know what is like to be rejected and misunderstood. These are experiences common to the general population. The problem in connection with not understanding really has to do with acceptance. It is one thing to be misunderstood, but it is far worse to be turned away as a result. Acceptance is not based purely on knowledge. Love, God's agape love, is unconditional acceptance.

A fear that may linger for years is that of being tempted by other men, even of being pursued by other gay men. This is most likely to happen, even repeatedly. The section at the end of Chapter 6, (Dealing with Gay Problems), gives help on dealing with this kind of dilemma. It is important for a wife to be alert to this possibility. An understanding, noncondemning wife can help defuse a potentially dangerous situation, thus deep and honest communication must be a regular part of a relationship. If a man can talk it out without jealousy arising from his wife, the temptation can be faced. If a woman tries to shield her husband from other men, disaster is near. A ball-and-chain is out of the question! Temptation cannot be prevented from happening; it can be turned from and resisted, talked out and prayed over. God's way is to love us through our temptations.

No temptation has overtaken you that is not common to man. God is faithful, and he will not let you be tempted beyond your strength, but with the temptation will also provide the way of escape, that you may be able to endure it. (1 Corinthians 10:13)

Notice that the temptation is not removed, but God gives power to endure. Love from a wife can supply much of that power.

TAKING THE INITIATIVE

A point often stressed by several men in our Love In Action ministry is that women must assume some initiative in lovemaking. This does not mean the woman is to be the aggressor; it is simply that she is not to be totally passive. The man probably will be insecure in his lovemaking technique and will appreciate some tangible help. The idea that a woman is to be passive in lovemaking is a cultural myth. There is no other reason for it. Biblically, there is nothing to suggest that the man is to instigate everything. A woman can be and should be as involved in leading as the man.

If a woman is too aggressive, however, the man may feel unimportant and the reduction to a passive role in lovemaking may make him feel non-masculine. The man must be sure to be initiating too, at least as much as the woman. Neither should force sex. Both must be loving and cooperate in showing affection and sensuality. A woman should encourage manliness and not attempt to force it.

To make it practical, a woman should assist the man into her. This can be accomplished by relaxing, spreading the legs sufficiently and using the hand to guide the penis into the vagina. Preceding actual intercourse is the kissing, hugging, and general sexual foreplay, during all of which a woman can be careful not to push or apply pressure. It is a kind of art that can only be developed. No doubt, it seems to many women that this is all too hard, that there is so much responsibility and things to avoid that it can never work out. Remember, it is a process, a learning experience. It is one day at a time baptized in love and forgiveness. Marriage requires grace poured out on top of more grace, commitment that overcomes petty irritations and momentary failures.

RESPECT YOUR HUSBAND

A gay man may worry about whether his wife respects him. Guilt is always a result of sin and guilt on top of guilt has a way of destroying one's sense of worth and personal integrity. It is essential, therefore, for a woman to be careful to lift her husband up. She must see him as a new creature in Christ with the old things not only in the past but forgiven and forgotten by God as well. She must be careful to not throw his past up to him or otherwise intimidate him by reflecting on his previous gay activities. Words can be very destructive, and she will want to display solidarity with him. This is especially important in a group setting, when other people are around. It should not be over-done or inappropriate. Respect is more of an attitude than anything else, a communication that says, "I love you, I am your wife, and I am proud to be with you. You are my man. I am your woman. It is you, my husband, to whom I am committed." This is communicated by dress, body language, and a quiet confidence that expresses well being. Respect is indispensable to mature love. A man needs to be looked up to, especially when he has been used to feeling fearful of and inferi-or to women, which some gay men will experience. This is especially true when the woman is heterosexual. Homosexuality is looked down upon generally and this, of course, contributes to a poor self image for a gay person. To look up to and respect your husband is solid loving.

It is good to be with a woman; it makes a man feel normal. To be in public and hold hands, or to be arm-in-arm, contributes to a sense of normalcy. The sex act itself helps a gay man feel good about himself; it helps make him feel like a man. What an incredible thing a wife can do for her husband. No one else can do this. It is a wonderful thing.

HONESTY

Honesty is an absolute requirement for a successful marriage. Hon-esty is the essential ingredient for effective communication. We lie to protect ourselves, but in marriage, we should have a sense of safety with the wife or husband that gives a freedom to tell the truth.

Honesty is not simply a case of not lying. Honesty is not repressing our real feelings, even when those inner truths may produce some tension. Honesty is bringing out the inner frustrations and complaints that are felt and may seem to be quite intangible. Both the gay man and the straight woman must do this. Anger should not be repressed. Too often, it comes out in violence or depression. We are told to "be angry but sin not; do not let the sun go down on your anger" (Ephe-sians 4:26). Simple, involuntary anger becomes sin when we allow it to build up. Ideally, points of friction are to be dealt with, as they occur, and are to be resolved before the end of the day. Repressed anger is dangerous and can be a factor in the destruction of a marriage. Withdrawing, not facing up to reality, is harmful because it prevents the kind of communication which can solve problems.

BE A BIBLICAL MAN

Every woman needs a Biblical man, a man who assumes loving authority. A husband is responsible for his wife. There is a mutual responsibility in marriage, but God sees the man as the head of the wife and expects him to be a minister to her (Ephesians 5:23). Scripture instructs, "Husbands, love your wives, as Christ loved the church and gave Himself up for her" (Ephesians 5:25). I am convinced there is no higher call than this for a husband. The cross is the expression of the depths of Jesus' love. A husband is asked by God to lay his life down for his wife. Love of this caliber sets the stage for the honest expression of those things that must be dealt with. Respect cannot help but be present, and the desire for a woman to please and satisfy her man will emerge in a natural way.

Loving is not an emotion or feeling; it is a commitment. It is a responsibility; it is even a command. Loving takes time; it is best to love someone a long time, as much time as we have days on this earth.

PROTECTING DIGNITY

A woman married to a gay man must be especially careful to protect her husband from possible scandal or accusations. In my opinion, it is always best when family and friends are aware of one's gay past. In Christ, we are made new and are no longer gay, thieves, liars, etc. But even when the immediate community knows of a gay past, it is not necessary to let every new acquaintance know, too. This must be decided upon by the husband and wife together. If the choice is to not let anyone know, whether family and friends, the wife or husband needs to respect such a mutual decision and diligently protect the husband's or wife's dignity.

NO RUSH TO THE ALTER

An important word to a straight woman is to avoid rushing to the alter. Someone coming from a gay background needs at least one year (and better yet, three years) of complete celibacy before marriage should occur. When a couple comes for counseling, this is one of our first recommendations. If either one falls into sexual sin during their engagement, it may be wise for the marriage be postponed for some period of time. He needs time to learn how to handle his sexual urges in a responsible way. Sexual integrity comes only through times of great stress and temptation. The re-learning process cannot be hurried. Sex no longer can be the answer for anger, rebellion, or a means of retaliation. Those who would short circuit this event do so at great risk to their marriage. It may be that an engagement should be broken if the man falls into gayness again. It may mean that the man does not really want to marry. Many gays desire marriage as a way of leaving homosexuality, or for a chance to have a family when they are not actually out of the gay life at all. Of course, if the non-gay woman is having sex with other men during the engagement, that engagement should be broken. Such sexual irresponsibility indicates there are significant problems that must be worked out at the very least. If two people desire to try to make a relationship work even after failure, marriage counseling is recommended.

Talking with a competent counselor is strongly recommended in any case. Marriage is too important to not take advantage of every help available.

THE WEDDING NIGHT

Pressure must be taken off the wedding night, and it is the woman who can best do this. From all the preceding chapters, many techniques in reducing pressure for sexual performance can be gleaned. The emphasis does not have to be on sex that first night or throughout a honeymoon. Intercourse may be put off for the entire honeymoon, if necessary. The process of sensate focusing can begin on the honeymoon. There is no rush. Love and marriage is more than sex.

It is most probable that intercourse will not take place that first night. In surveying successful marriages involving an ex-gay, we find that many days, weeks, and even months pass before intercourse is a reality.

At this point, however, the gay man must not take advantage of his inability to achieve erection and leave his wife unsatisfied. As wives can be callous to their husband's needs during the menstrual period, so husbands can be self-centered and inconsiderate when unable to achieve erection. This is a time when love is tested. If the gay man truly loves his wife, he will certainly desire to fulfill her and satisfy her. Since, in the female, the pleasure zone surrounds the clitoris, gently massaging this area will usually bring the wife to orgasm. Most women do not want the clitoris directly stimulated by the hand. The fingers are usually too rough for comfort. One of the most pleasing things a man can do is to gently rub his flaccid penis against the clitoris. The softness of the glans penis provides stimulation, somewhat equivalent to the tongue. A man may be pleasing his wife to a greater degree in this manner than if he had a full erection and was engaging in intercourse.

If perchance the husband can achieve full erection, he should not prolong sex on the first night if his wife is a virgin. It is best to come quickly to climax, and then stimulate the wife to orgasm manually to protect her from soreness.

Should the couple opt for the use of condoms, it should be the wife who places the condom on her husband. Nothing is more frustrating than attempting to unroll a condom during sex play. Condoms are best used when there is a problem of premature ejaculation. If a wife insists on their use when no problem exists, she may be erecting an unseen barrier in the marriage, as many men dislike condoms.

The gay man must keep in mind that a woman is different from a man and needs an extended period of foreplay. It seems that a gay man who always used to ask his partner, "What do you like?" somehow never thinks to ask his wife the same question. As stated many times already, communication is vital to a good marriage. The husband must explore his wife, just as he previously explored other men. He should ask her what feels good and be attentive to her response.

A man should avoid forcing his penis into his wife's vagina. It is best to wait until she indicates she is ready to receive it. Many men mistake the moistening of the vagina area as meaning the wife is ready for penetration, but this is not always the case. It may be some time after this point that full engorgement takes place and the vagina has tightened and is ready to receive the penis. The husband should wait for his wife to guide him in. One of the most frequent complaints of women is that men are bunglers—they penetrate before a woman is ready. They may cause pain for the woman in the attempt, and then rush to a climax before the woman has reached the plateau stage. A husband must learn to love his wife, not use and abuse her. A review of I Corinthians 13 is advisable and certainly applies well to marital sex.

If the man wants a loving response to his sexual advances, he must be considerate in the area of hygiene. This means a clean body, close shave, fresh breath, and trimmed nails on the toes and fingers. The gay man has usually spent much time preparing himself for gay sex, and now is not the time for him to give up these important considerations.

As the marriage progresses, do not let routine rob the marriage of its vitality. Gay men sometimes have sex in the afternoon and the term "matinee" is heard in gay circles. Remember occasionally to have a "matinee." She will enjoy the diversion.

IN-LAWS AND PARENTS

This area is so intricate it seems impossible to make a competent presentation. It may be a subject best dealt with in counseling.

In-laws can destroy a marriage, and it is precisely here that the Word of God must be heeded. *"Therefore a man leaves his father and his mother and cleaves to his wife, and they become one flesh"* (Genesis 2:24). My emphasis is on "a man leaves his father and mother." This applies to the woman as well. Emotional emancipation is a must for a new life in marriage. Both the man and woman must deal with this issue honestly and carefully.

A gay man may not want his in-laws to know of his gay past. If they clearly do not know, it is best to let this condition stand as long as it is mutually agreeable. It may be necessary to stand aloof from in-laws if they insist on interfering. Clear headed evaluation is necessary here. Marriage means a transfer of allegiance and loyalty from the parents to the husband or wife. Respect for parents continues, but the child has become and adult and now submits to the husband or wife. A couple may be quick to say their in-laws and parents are no problem. This is rarely true, however. Of course, emancipation is a process and requires the establishing of a new security system. The people I have noticed to be the most successful in this regard are those whose security is based on Jesus Christ. When Jesus is first, then human relationships are more likely to be in proper order.

GAY MAN—GAY WOMAN

Most of the points discussed under the previous section have application here, and I will repeat many things, rather than stick to only original material.

By gay, I mean ex-gay, a person from a gay background. Unfortunately, even though a person may be a "new creature in Christ," there is much that remains the very same. In the case of homosexuality, the factor that usually hangs on is psychic response. Therefore, sexuality continues to be a problem, even when overt homosexual behavior is rejected. A glance at the marriage section in a Christian bookstore shows that heterosexuals have a dozen or so books to read if desired. Heterosexuals have their problems, of course—I did. The value of this manual is that it addresses the gay person directly with special consideration.

THE BIGGEST RISK

A gay man marrying a gay woman may seem the ultimate in troubles, but from several angles, it may be the best of the three possibilities. In terms of understanding and acceptance, especially the latter, having been present makes a lot of difference. There is likely to be a higher degree of tolerance and patience between two ex-gay people. One of the major fears of the gay is not being understood and fearing the straight person will not be respecting. The relationship of two former homosexuals has the potentiality of being more compatible than either of the other combinations.

COUNSEL

Pre-marital counseling is a valuable experience. If either person rejects counsel, then the relationship is in danger. By counsel I do not necessarily mean a professional that charges $150 an hour. A mature and knowledgeable minister may be fine, although a sex therapist may be of considerable help. Any money spent on counsel will be money well spent. Every avenue should be explored. The dividends will show up in the family life later on.

JUST FOR CHILDREN

In not advisable for two gay people marry simply so they can have children. Marriage is undertaken due to the love that two people have for each other. "Arrangements" will not do. Yes, it is a major drive to have children, but kids need a strong family with parents who love each other and have a normal relationship. This may work for parents, both of whom come from a gay background. This can be a delicate situation and require careful consideration. Children are not playthings; they are persons who need every opportunity to grow up to be happy and healthy.

On the other hand, children may not be wanted at all, and this is understandable. Children do not make a marriage. In fact, they may be the undoing of a relationship. Children are a major change and require a great deal of time and energy, not to mention money. My counsel is to wait at least one year, two is even better, before even beginning to have children. When children come, things change forever. Every couple, gay background or not, should first give themselves time to grow together and learn to love one another alone.

SEXUAL CONCERNS

One issue is body hair. Obviously, a gay woman may react to the hair of the man and the man to the hairlessness of the woman. There is potential for tension here. Hair, we need to remember, is natural. Compromises may need to be made. A woman may let her body hair grow to please the man, if this is requested. Or the man may react to a woman not shaving. For adequate solutions to be given here, much more information would be required in particular situations. This is certainly a topic that counseling could deal with.

Body hair, or the lack of it, may be a problem only at first. Time makes a difference and areas that were troublesome at first gradually decrease in intensity and importance. Basically, I counsel adjusting to that which is normal in terms of the culture. Here I mean the woman shaving, but if either desire it the other way, then let that need rule. Fetishes can be broken down through the normalcy of marriage.

There, of course, is the issue about sex. Sensate focusing or pleasuring may be good to employ right from the honeymoon. Mutual masturbation can also be used. It is not necessary to begin having intercourse right away. Intercourse for two ex-gays may be highly traumatizing for one or both. Oral sex may be much appreciated by each but difficult or perhaps impossible to give by one or both parties. Giving oral sex may be the one thing that most offends, because it is the most "opposite" to the previous lifestyle. Tender loving care is very necessary at this point.

Anal sex is to be examined and considered. Many, if not most, women have trouble with it, though some enjoy it. Women from a gay background may strongly object, so it should be done only if it is clearly desired by both people.

It is understood for sex for both people may be disappointing at first. Neither may know how to properly love the opposite sex and sex performance may not nearly match previous gay sex. The man will have to learn to take his time and make love for a much longer time than he has been used to. The woman may be fearful of the penis and the man fearful of, or repulsed by, the woman's genitals, which seem more mysterious to the man than the penis is to the woman. Each person will have to give the other person and themselves a good measure of grace, and forgiveness may have to flow like a mighty river.

Sex should not occupy center stage. It has an important place for sure, but it is not central. Love is central and sex is only one way of expressing love. A relaxed attitude toward sex in an atmosphere of other-centeredness will certainly help take the pressure off performing. Both persons in an ex-gay marriage will be concerned about performing and will be worried about being able to enjoy sex and please the other. These are understandable fears. There are no magic solutions or tricks to make them all go away. They are worked out through as a process of growing in the face of hard times. It is here that the grace of God must be grasped; this is a time to forgive, a time for courage, and a time for prayer.

Then there is the issue about who should lead. In the discussion on the combination of a gay man and a straight woman, I emphasized the need for the woman to take a considerable amount of initiative in sex, everything from kissing and hugging to guiding the man into her. This need not be overdone, though, lest the man feel he is unimportant in the whole process. However, at this juncture, the man is going to need to take the initiative. It may not always hold true, but in general, when male/female roles are fairly "even," it would be most natural for the man to assume the lead. (I can imagine some readers questioning this point.)

There are so many potential exceptions that it is best for the couple to openly discuss the question of leading in sex. Perhaps this point is suitable for examination in the counseling office.

Then there are fetishes and partialisms. A fetish is a non-sexual stimulant that has become, by some unknown process, necessary for sexual excitement. For example, army boots may provoke strong sexual arousal. Or, women's garments worn by a man may be a sexual stimulant. A partialism is related to some part of the human body, i.e., hair patterns, feet, armpits, etc. It is a focal point that somehow represents the entire person and like a fetish, provokes strong desire. The word partialism is little known, and the word fetish is generally used to refer to both animate and inanimate objects.

Gay men more often have sexual fetishes than women, but gay women may also have them. Any fetish must be openly revealed and discussed before marriage. Most fetishes are harmless and will be continued with little problem, but others may be absolutely impossible—for instance, when violence is involved. In the case of partialism, if it involves another man's back, then a woman's back will be a turn-off. In this case and others like it, the problem must be worked out honestly and openly. A couple can determine if a fetish or partialism is acceptable or impossible and work from there.

ROLE REVERSALS

A gay woman who has been used to taking the male role in gayness may need to reverse her role to the feminine or more passive stance. I know this is delicate ground, and there will be strong opinions on both sides of this issue. A woman may not be able to change roles, and a man who has been accustomed to being the "fem" in gay relationships may not be able to achieve any significant change, either. The question then becomes, is it wrong for the man to be passive and the woman aggressive?

My opinion is that it is okay for the normal roles to be reversed if the following are true: one, both people are in total, honest agreement that this is how it should be; two, there are to be no children (such role reversal would be damaging to a child); and three, if the continuing roles that were characteristic of gayness would keep the door open to, or contribute to, a future return to gayness. Repentance and clear cut moving out of homosexuality may necessitate abandoning what might be affected roles. This is a complex issue, and it may be next-to-impossible for anyone but a truly qualified counselor to give a sure word on it.

Roles do not just come and go with a quick decision. It may take years to unlearn old patterns and relearn new ones. However, when a person thoroughly extricates himself/herself from the gay life, many affectations and role characteristics fall off simply because they are no longer needed. Yet, new roles are not easy to learn if there is no role model. This is one reason the community of the church is important, because there will be persons within it that can be examples to learn from. Normalcy grows as we submit ourselves to it.

PERPETUATING WEAK POINTS

It would be appropriate to see the film "A Different Kind of Story" as an illustration of this point. The movie depicts two gay people who begin to fall in love and are compatible only as their neurotic needs are filled by the other. Actually, each one was encouraging the weak points of the other, fusing the character traits that were harmful in the first place. This is always the danger in a relationship between a gay man and a gay woman. Both people have excessive needs, needs that are legitimate in one sense, but some of which are a direct outcome of gayness and are best rejected. Of course, this consideration applies to all three marriage combinations, but is most obvious here. A marriage should be liberating and a move toward normalcy, not a compounding of problems.

We as people are notoriously shortsighted when it comes to our friends and those we love. No one, it seems, can tell us anything. It is sometimes comical but tragic in other instances. If only we would allow a concerned outsider to evaluate the dynamics of a relationship, many hurts could be avoided. It is far better to suffer a broken heart than to continue a relationship that may prove to be a genuine mess. Anyone who is afraid of a counselor giving an objective evaluation is going about things in the wrong way. Truth and goodness are always able to survive in the light of day and can stand the test of righteous judgment. Occasionally, in our Love in Action ministry, two people will start up a relationship that the leaders can easily see is wrong, yet the people involved will reject counsel. The bad relationships seem to always have this happen. Good solid relationships work the other way. The people submit themselves to counsel and are eager for evaluation. In a bad relationship, a kind of stubborn rebellion settles upon the people involved, and even though they know what they are doing is wrong, they are unwilling to admit it. Their response is to "dig in," persist in the relationship and begin to exclude themselves from other friends. In time, the relationship usually ends. A relationship must be upbuilding, not simply perpetuating weak points. Two people who seem to fit hand-and-glove may be needing just the opposite, a relationship with someone who challenges them and causes them to change.

WISHFUL THINKING

Some people are solidly out of the gay life while others are barely out. A person who is securely out of gayness must be careful to develop a relationship with someone who is also securely out. There is no place for wishful thinking in this regard, such as imagining that a person is really out when it is obvious they are not. It is suggested that one year of celibacy is essential on the part of both people. My counsel is to "see with both eyes," to use careful discernment and develop a relationship only with someone who has demonstrated they are out of the gay life and intend to remain so.

A danger that exists when both the man and the woman are ex-gay is that if one goes back into gayness after a failure in the relationship, the other may also. If this prospect is acknowledged, the more likely such a defeat will not happen. Idealism will need to be rejected. We are sinners and anything is possible. A solid, even radical commitment to Christ is essential for the gay person (or for anyone, for that matter) if quality love and positive growing are to occur in one's relationships.

Marriage must not be entered into as a ministry with the purpose of keeping someone out of gayness by making him/her heterosexual. It simply will not work. The idea that "My love will make the difference" is shallow and contrary to reality. It is a form of self deception and will lead only to disappointment. It is better never to have loved at all, than to love unwisely. Love is not an overwhelming heartthrob, characterized by goose bumps and tingly sensations, any more than it is determined by a closed mind and cold, rigid facts. Love can be wise and centered in reality; in fact, it must be that way to survive. People are not to be treated as objects to be used for our own personal satisfaction.

POSSESSIVENESS

Closing the deal quickly is good for salespersons, but not for people moving toward marriage. Time makes for fine wines, and the same is true for marriages. People who are rushing their engagement or a commitment to marriage are going too fast. An insecure person wants to nail it down, to get a decision that binds rather than allows love to grow naturally. Possessiveness is a sure danger signal and must be resisted. It takes months at least to know a person well enough to love them. Anything less than one year of being together is far too short a time for a solid love relationship to be built.

FIGHTS

Fighting is unavoidable. Two people who are closely united are bound to clash from time to time. Even the best of marriages experience periodic misunderstandings and conflict. But fights between two people who have come out of gayness could be more damaging than normal.

People sometimes lose their heads in a fight and use extremely derogatory terms. Where an ex-gay is involved, words such as "fag", "dyke" and "queer" can become highly effective weapons. This is dirty fighting (but understandable), since one gay knows how to get at another gay person in the most serious way. Knowing this will help soften the blow.

Words are one thing, but there is something worse. Fights may provoke self pity and a desire to return to gay life. Such a reaction may be calculated to "pay back" or is done out of a wounded ego. There is no way to prevent all fights, but fights may cause a person to return to what is familiar. Of course, going back to gayness is an immature reaction. The psychology surrounding this is highly complex. To forewarn is the best I can do under these circumstances.

If, during the engagement period, one or the other person goes back into gayness, the engagement should be broken. Sexual stability and integrity are absolutely essential elements for a successful marriage.

PROTECTIVE DIGNITY

Two people must decide on whether they want to expose their gay pasts. Pressures are lessened when there can be complete openness, but this may not always be possible. It is best when such a decision can be made apart from fears and insecurity. The future of the marriage should be the determining factor. If love will be served by not exposing past gayness, then that is right. There would have to be some rather extenuating circumstances in order to keep it all quiet, especially in regard to parents, in-laws, and children. Of course, geography makes a difference. In the San Francisco Bay Area, the climate is better for gays and ex-gays than some other places. This matter must be talked about and prayed over carefully.

In-laws, if they know about the gayness, must not be allowed to interfere and make judgments. Emotional emancipation is a quality of maturity that is as valuable as gold in a marriage. If it is not there, the parents and in-laws may make life miserable. On occasion, some drastic actions may be necessary, such as telling some people what they can and can't do, or even moving away.

WEDDING NIGHT

An ex-gay couple is likely to have an interesting wedding night. I hope no one is offended by that sentence. I mean they will enjoy a lovely and very wonderful wedding night, whether sex happens or not. Sex should be de-emphasized in favor of sacrificial loving. Self and mutual masturbation is a good beginning, as is initiating sensate focusing. A honeymoon can be an exciting adventure, and the wedding night need not be spent in a motel with a big bed dominating the room. The wedding night is the first night spent together and should happen as both desire it to.

STRAIGHT MAN—GAY WOMAN

There is material in this section concerning the woman that could have been included in the preceding section but seems to especially fit when a straight man is involved who may not understand gayness like a gay man would. The critical element in the straight man—gay woman union is the woman. She will have to suffer or change the most, and therefore will need to receive an extra amount of tender, loving care.

EASY DOES IT

This slogan from Alcoholics Anonymous fits well here, and is counsel the straight man must grasp. Pressure for affection, a short engagement, and sex is likely to produce real trouble. A man must step back occasionally and give a woman freedom and opportunity to evaluate. A woman from a gay background, especially if she has been exposed to the women's right movement, may have resentments built up toward men and may believe that a man wants only one thing. She may have trouble believing a man can be tender and loving. A man must be loving but not too soft; he must be firm and manly. The macho style will not be appreciated and will be rejected in most cases. Gay men have often developed resentments toward women, especially if part of their gayness is in reaction to their mothers. But the groups involving gay men do not war against women, like many feminist groups war against men. Also, many gay women have been molested or raped, resulting in both fear and hatred towards men. It may take a long period of time to work through hostile feelings and anxieties. To do so, a man must be loving and patient, with a willingness to lay his life down for the woman he loves. "Easy does it" is appropriate counsel for the straight man who should keep in mind that it is better to give than to receive.

A man must be careful not to manhandle or push a woman around. After marriage, the sexual part must be low pressure for the woman, also. She is most vulnerable and must feel that she will not be violated. There may be a strong tendency for a woman to feel that sexual intercourse with a man is an attack on her person and an actual violation. She may fear that she is losing her identity.

SEXUAL MATTERS

A man must allow his wife to be celibate at times. The Bible allows it for prayer (1 Corinthians 7:5), and, of course, is an option at any time. A woman is not less sexual than a man, but her need may be for a space of time when she can choose to be celibate. Also, many women want no sex during their menstrual period. This must be honored. During the menstrual period, self and mutual masturbation is an acceptable choice. A woman in her period may be easily upset and irritable, and any sex may be repulsive to her. It may be a time for total abstinence.

A gay woman may have difficulty giving oral sex, but may enjoy receiving it. A penis in the face may be troublesome, since it is the strongest possible confrontation with male sexuality.

Good communication is essential in sex. Not only is sex talk during intercourse helpful as well as exciting, but it helps the other person know what pleases and what does not. Do not say you like something when you do not, or you will simply get more of it. A person must be honest as to likes and dislikes and have the courage to voice it.

If a woman has trouble accepting the penis, a vibrator may be helpful. It can reduce the fear of penetration, but probably a finger is better.

A gay woman may not want to shave her underarms and legs, although this is not true for all gay women. The woman will need to be open about her desires and feelings and the man understanding and tolerant. The presence or absence of hair is not critical, but the matter needs to be treated with loving consideration.

CHILDREN

Some gay women fear pregnancy and may not want to become pregnant. If this is the case, marriage is still possible, of course, but the man will have to seriously deal with what it means to him to not have children. If he wants children and it is clear that she does not, perhaps there should be no marriage. Any idea that the woman will change her mind, or that she can be tricked into getting pregnant, is an serious mistake and perverse thinking. In any case, a woman's feelings about pregnancy and children should be thoroughly discussed and taken very seriously.

A woman may want children, but fear having a family at the same time. Her own childhood could have been such that she does not want to bring children into a hostile world. Another possibility is that she may want children, but pregnancy is too "female" for her. She may be used to taking the male role in gayness and have resentments toward feminism in general. If there seems to be any complications regarding children, I suggest finding competent counsel in order to work out the problem.

BUILDING FEMININITY

A gay woman may need to be built up as a woman. Gayness may contribute to a depreciation of femaleness. Adequate acceptance of what it means to be feminine is essential for a woman in marriage. She may never be, nor is it necessarily good to be, fashioned after a Vogue magazine model, but men do need a woman to be womanly. Femininity in its most natural form brings out normal masculinity in men. It works both ways and for a healthy self image, a woman needs to be treated as a woman. Femininity may cause confusion; some women hate it and some long for it. A man can complement a woman on her femininity and relate to her in time honored manners that treat a woman with respect. Affection and gifts are also helpful, particularly affection.

THE SELF-ASSURED MAN

A gay woman needs a man, a person who has a quiet confidence about himself. The macho image is a thin veneer for insecurity or even latent homosexuality. The macho style must be rejected. It is manly to be sensitive and considerate, and being a man has nothing to do with muscles or body size. A man who has confidence in himself as a man is at peace with himself. He takes authority without having to fight for it. He does not have to dominate or control, but leads by example and love. However, he can be stern and direct when necessary. Some gay women have never known or personally related to a male figure and consequently time is needed for appreciation to grow. It is not good for a man to be a doormat. A gay woman may test a man to see if she can get away with wearing the pants. If she can, she will likely turn cool to the relationship or begin to resent the man's weakness. It may be that a woman will go through many ups and downs before she can work through negative reactions to men that she may have developed in her gay life, and also before she can begin responding as the woman God made her to be.

SUBMISSION

Submission has become a dirty word in recent years. It provokes serious debate in women's rights groups when the word is used to describe a wife's relationship to her husband. Some women have dismissed the Bible and Christianity all together because of Paul's teaching on the submission of a wife to her husband. I am going to quote several key verses in order to facilitate a brief discussion on the matter.

> Be subject to one another out of reverence for Christ. Wives, be subject to your husbands, as to the Lord. For the husband is the head of the church, his body, and is himself its savior. As the church is subject to Christ, so let wives also be subject in

everything to their husbands. Husbands, love your wives, as Christ loved the church and gave himself up for her. (Ephesians 5:21–25)

The opening statement, "Be subject to one another" is the key phrase. Submission is a mutual responsibility, and the husband is also to submit or be subject to his wife. The proper translation is "subject" rather than "submission." "Subject" carries the idea of support and cooperation. It is not a demeaning posture. It is the reverse of rebellion and opposition. It is a working together, united in action so there may be peace and prosperity.

Paul says the husband is the head of the family and the head over his wife. He likens the headship of the man to the woman to the relationship between Christ and the church. There is always a head or leader in a healthy, ordered enterprise. If there is no clearly established leader in a family, there will be tension, fighting, and a general atmosphere of chaos. No man can lead without permission from those who recognize his leadership and willing cooperate with it. In any grouping of two or more people, one will emerge as the leader. God has established the husband as the head of the family and so there does not need to be a power struggle. The husband must assume his God-appointed place as leader and the wife must allow him this, even encourage him to do it. If this does not happen, the children will have poor role models to learn from and could grow up confused about who they are. Also, if the husband does not function as the head in a Christ-like way, it will be harder for the wife to recover from her gayness. If a woman refuses to acknowledge the Scripture and rejects any attempt for the man to be the leader, the relationship will not wok (or will be a neurotic one at best). It is hoped that a model of mutuality will be developed where there is cooperative, joint leadership. For a man to be the head does not mean mutuality is impossible. There can develop a spontaneous flowing that is not laborious or contrived. But, given who we are and the world we live in, it will take time and work.

God's way of being subject to one another is designed for the peace and security of the family. Often God's plans cause us to rebel when we hear them since we are a rebellious race of people. Our hearts must be yielded to the Lordship of Jesus Christ before we can genuinely follow the teachings of the Bible.

LOSS OF IDENTITY

A woman most often suffers the loss of her last name in marriage. We are seeing that this is not automatic now. I mean that women are retaining their family name or combining it with that of her husband's. The first scenario can be quite traumatic to her and may threaten her with a loss of identity. In marriage, some women sense they will be demeaned by becoming a "Mrs. Somebody," a "Mrs. John Doe." There is also the fear of belonging to someone to the point you are no longer your own person.

Some gay women feel they were cheated by being born female, and to be stuck with "Mrs." may seem like a curse. Control may be the key problem because a woman who is fearful of losing her identity in a marriage may be concerned with being controlled. "Mrs." may mean loss of identity but may also mean being trapped in a subservient position that is sanctioned by God, our culture, and by other people. This fear should be openly aired if it is present with assurances given and principles established. "Mrs." does not mean loss of identity or control. The blending of two names to one is a reality. Certainly, the oneness of a family should be reflected in financial matters in that the finances are mutual assets and there is one joint bank account. Such measures reflect that a single unit exists and there is mutual trust. Marriage is commitment and each reservation weakens commitment.

MARRIAGE FOR LIFE

Marriage is not an experiment. It is not to be tried for a while to see if it works. Two people should know each other well enough prior to marriage to have already worked through many problems. Many people feel that marriage will solve problems. However, the reverse is often true; marriage may actually compound existing troubles. Marriage must be seen as a lifelong commitment, although divorce is possible if all else absolutely fails. Marriage is not a prison any more than it is a temporary relationship.

PRE-MARITAL SEX

I decided to discuss pre-marital sex in this section, rather than the others, because I feel it is more likely to be a problem in the straight man—gay woman combination than in either of the other two. The gay male is likely to be more reluctant to engage in sex with a woman than a non-gay male. Since the male is usually more aggressive than the female (at least in our society), pre-marital sex would be more likely to occur in the case of a straight man. One of my favorite slogans is, "Sex ruins friendships." A relationship can be flowering, with the two people learning to know and appreciate each other. Then sex enters the picture, and the scene is drastically altered. Courtship should be free from sex; sex belongs in marriage. Being one flesh before the love is settled and matured will put a shadow on the relationship that could easily destroy it. There also remains the truth that pre-marital sex is breaking God's law regarding fornication (see Matthew 15:19). Paul wrote, *"For this is the will of God, your sanctification: that you abstain from immorality"* (1 Thessalonians 4:3). The word "immorality" is "porneia" in the Greek which means fornication or all sexuality outside of marriage.

Sex is difficult enough without playing with it outside the supportive structure of marriage. Guilt is a powerful force, as is lack of trust and respect. Yet, someone might think that especially when one person is ex-gay, it would be good to be sure that the sexual relationship is going to work. My answer is this: fornication will not be the same as sex within marriage, and is no test at all. If sex is going to be difficult, it should occur only within the context of the strong love commitment of marriage. In any case, simply having sex is not all there is to love, and to try sex before marriage (as if that were the major element of marriage) is to misunderstand both sex and marriage. I am not just concerned that no one sin; rather, the success of a marriage is the issue. On the one hand, we have the Biblical command, and on the other, we have personal concern. In this case, they match up to produce a very strong case for abstaining from fornication.

The pressure on a gay woman for sex from a straight man would very likely be the wrong thing and could jeopardize the entire relationship. It would reinforce any idea on the woman's part that men want only one thing. Sex in such an insecure atmosphere will probably be a failure and produce nothing but disappointing experiences. There will be plenty of time for sex when it is right.

The passage previously quoted from Paul is followed by counsel on how to "take" a wife: *"that each one of you know how to take a wife for himself in holiness and honor, not in the passion of lust like heathen who do not know God"* (1 Thessalonians 4:4–5).

THE WEDDING NIGHT

The man must be careful to be extremely considerate to his wife on the wedding night. It is here that the gay woman may feel most fearful and under the control of the man. She must have freedom to enter into the planning for the wedding night. It is best to let her decide how it shall be, or at least, she should be able to draw a line when she feels she must. The wedding night should not be a traumatic event, but a carefree adventure to which there are no threatening monsters attached. To reiterate an important point, intercourse does not have to happen right away. In some instances, it can take months to reach that point. However, mutual and self-masturbation can be enjoyed, coupled with hugging and closeness. The process of sensate focusing can be employed, with Phases I and II lasting for many days each. The wedding night and the honeymoon, as well as the whole of married life, can be a creative adventure in regard to sexuality.

BEING BIBLICAL PEOPLE

The man may assume his place as head of the family and not force his wife to do so. It is biblical that this be the pattern, but this does not preclude that a couple will work out how it is for them to relate to each other. Mutuality works well. Marriage is not a boss-employer relationship. My view is that for a couple to work toward the biblical model, a wife will encourage her husband to be a leader, and the kind she can support and encourage in that role.

SUFFERING

Marriage for an ex-gay person may cause some suffering, even a great deal of it. Marriage for anyone is going to mean some suffering. That is reality. The positive aspect of suffering is first, that it produces endurance and second, develops character and maturity. Maturity yields hope, the kind of hope that withstands adversity successfully. Paul presents this process in Romans 5:3–5. Suffering is a part of life and if we learn to run and escape it, we will never grow up. If in pursuing love that leads to marriage, suffering is encountered, we should walk through it by faith, thank God for it, and seek to grow from it. No good marriage just happens. Marriages are built slowly and painstakingly with prayer and grace.

6

Growing a Marriage

L ove is like a living organism—it grows. But it grows slowly, and takes time, years of time, to grow into all that it can be. On a practical level this means that two people will have to be patient and, like good farmers, provide for their marriage a rich soil in which love can be nurtured. Dating, engagement, honeymoon—these are merely simple beginnings, points of a journey and there are yet many miles to experience.

Weeds grow quickly, but redwoods take a while longer. The same is true of a good marriage. In some instances, I have seen ten years or ever longer pass before a relationship flourished, not that it was dismal prior to coming into maturity. But reality shows us that as love grows, so a marriage grows. This chapter is intended to provide some material on how to go about "growing" a marriage. Personally, I am in the process myself and, of course, I do not have all the answers. But eighteen years of being in the front lines have taught me something, and nearly as instructive have been years of pastoral counseling.

Perhaps the basic point can now be stated: a good marriage must be diligently pursued, because it requires hard work. Although this hard work is needed, it is not impossible work, and very slowly the marriage will grow and develop. It does not simply happen, any more than buying lumber is all that is needed to build a house. There is an analogy that exists between building a house and building a marriage, with the foundations, floors, walls, ceilings, etc.

Too many times have I seen young, married Christians get so caught up in their new lives together that they neglect Christ and the church. This is not healthy. They begin building their careers, buying a house, buying cars and furniture, and God, who had brought them

126

that far, is neglected, though indirectly. Please hear me on this point; grow in Christ at all costs. Founding a marriage on dreams, goals, even love itself, will not do. I am reminded of the parable of the two houses in Matthew 7:24. Jesus said, *"Great was the fall thereof"* in speaking of the house build on sand. Start with rock as a solid foundation and continue building with rock.

WHAT IS LOVE?

Love is an act of the will. There is chemistry, a sexual interest and romance, but the core is a choice to be committed. Argue with that point and you are in trouble. Feelings come and go; there are biological phases, stages of life, even gravity, and they all affect us. If love is grounded only in our heart and not also in our head and will, love well be compromised and the marriage along with it.

Saying "I do" is going to have to be the result of a determination to make it work, to love no matter what. Tenaciousness is a wonderful quality; it is putting the hand to the plow and not looking back.

Love is commitment; love is laying your life down for your husband or wife. The model for us to follow is Jesus and His cross, and the way He gave up His life for us. Paul's word to husbands is, *"Husbands, love your wives, as Christ loved the church and gave Himself up for her"* (Ephesians 5:25). Scripture puts the more radical commitment on the husband as the head, the protector, the one who is to "cover" his wife. Love is the willingness to lay down one's life. To lay down one's life is a daily dying to one's own interests and making the sacrifices necessary for a marriage to grow. I am not using these strong words casually. I am aware of their import and severity, but they must be presented so that we may follow them. Since the Holy Spirit has inspired Paul's words in Ephesians 5, God intends for us to live them and so will empower us to work them out in our lives.

Love means sacrificing. Every husband and every wife will have to expend himself/herself to meet the needs of the other. No self-centered person will survive very well in a marriage. To make it practical, sacrifice might be looked at in terms of adjustment. All of us develop any number of peculiarities that we alone find acceptable. Habits such as throwing our clothes about, leaving the soap on the shower floor, or not liking peas or cabbage, etc., may need to be adjusted. This is tangible laying down of one's life. Adjusting for the reason of love is real love.

Love is welcoming. There is a beautiful verse that expresses what I mean. It is, *"Welcome one another, therefore, as Christ has welcomed you, for the glory of God"* (Romans 14:7).

Consider how Jesus welcomed us. Imagine two people, each welcoming the other into their lives. Almost no words can be found to express the magnificence of such a love. There is only one love that could be more highly sought for. The returns of this welcoming love are incalculable. Jesus welcomed us unconditionally, with our ugly sin sticking out all over. Agape love, loving in spite of, is always going to work, and it can be present in a marriage through God's grace. It is a gift from God and comes to us through loving God first and best. It is a love that filters down from God to us and then through us to others.

THE ESSENTIAL INGREDIENT

What is the essential component of a marriage? The answer can only be this: **forgiveness**.

There are going to be fights. Disagreements surface in any marriage if it is anything close to normal. Fights are a reality. When there are none, something is wrong. Someone is repressing his or her feelings, and communication is not taking place. It is much better to express yourself, even if a fight results. Thus, forgiveness is a very necessary part of any marriage.

There are several things that forgiveness is not. It is not toleration. Tolerating behavior or circumstances that are wrong and are doing damage will allow resentment and bitterness to grow. It solves nothing to meekly or determinedly allow the status quo to go unchallenged when it should be confronted. Tolerating bad behavior, instead of dealing with it, is like a long, slow fuse attached to a dozen sticks of dynamite. This is true for both husbands and wives.

Forgiveness is not keeping score. Forgiveness is being willing to not bring up the argument again. There may be solutions to arguments, but no forgiveness is occurring. One characteristic of God's grace is that He forgets our sin, as well as forgiving it. Satan is the one who accuses us, not God. God does not throw our past back in our faces. The blood of Christ covers us. Of course, unfortunately, we do not forget the injustices, the reasons and the cruel words. Often our minds refuse to forget, even when we try. We may not be able to forget, but we can forgive. Forgiveness is a choice and an act. The past has got to remain in the past. Fights need to be fair.

Forgiveness is a decision we make. Though we cannot forget the trouble, we do not retaliate or act out. Being lovey-dovey is no substitute for forgiveness. Sex is not to be used as a reward. Forgiveness is honest; it is a recognition of wrong on the one hand and a decision to be reconciled on the other. Problems do not go away with a few kisses. Problems must be viewed realistically and reduced through understanding, resolution, and ultimately forgiveness.

Forgiveness is rarely a one-sided affair. In most troubled human enterprises, no one is perfect and beyond blame. Problems are resolved when both people give and receive forgiveness. When one person refuses to identify his/her own responsibility, there can be no genuine reconciliation. We must be discerning and look beyond the immediate confusion to the influences and causes that led to the current outburst. I have not seen too many innocent parties in marital disputes.

Forgiveness is not a nursing a hard heart. Sometimes a pseudo-forgiveness will be affected. For the sake of peace in the house, differences and hurts will simply be overlooked. One person may believe there has been a resolution, but in fact, the other person has chosen to remain quiet and hide an unyielded stony heart. Probably great spiritual and psychological damage will be the result of this hard heartedness. Honesty must be central in forgiveness. Hiding reality for altruistic or political reasons is dangerous and ineffectual in dealing with problems.

Forgiveness does not always flow from our feelings or our "heart." Forgiveness comes from our will, that part of us where decisions are made. Our will acts as a result of our understanding that forgiveness is essential if two people are going to be able to continue together. Jesus tells us to forgive, and He can tell us to because of His Lordship in our lives:

> *Then Peter came up and said to Him, "Lord, how often shall my brother sin against me, and I forgive him? As many as seven times?" Jesus said to him, "I do not say to you seven times, but seventy times seven."*   Matthew 18:21, 22

This is quite clear. There is no limit to forgiveness in terms of numbers of times. Forgiveness can be motivated, if all else fails, from the desire to obey Christ. It is impossible to love and not forgive. When we consider the love of God as seen in the Cross of Jesus, it is plain how love is bound up with forgiveness.

Forgiveness is not to be an occasional experience—It must be a daily occurrence. Years ago, I was struck by Dietrich Bonhoeffer's thoughts on forgiveness, as he expressed them in a wedding sermon when his sister was marrying his best friend, Ebhard Bethge. I incorporated the essence of his words into the wedding sermon I use as a pastor. Bonhoeffer said, with some rearranging on my part:

> You are to live together in the forgiveness of your sins, for without it no human fellowship, least of all a marriage, can survive. Don't insist on your rights; don't blame each other; don't judge or condemn each other; don't find fault with each other. But take on another as you are, and forgive each other every day from the bottom of your hearts. From the first day of your marriage until the last your rule must be: "Receive one another...to the praise of God."

HOW TO FIGHT

When I do marriage counseling, I always ask people how they fight. They are surprised. I tell them to not get married until they have had at least one fight (or even better, more than one). Why?

People will fight; we all do, as you know. Sometimes the closer we get the more we fight until we mature a bit.

The main thing is how we fight because there are healthy and destructive ways to fight.

Of course, violence and physical damage is not good and will hopefully not even enter the picture. If there is violence and recurring abuse, it is vital that counsel be sought. Understandably, pride is involved; it is so hard to face up to such things. The shame is considerable and to think of opening up to another person, even a counselor, is scary. Yet, it must be done.

There is something worse than violence: withdrawal. There is no more destructive way to fight than refusing to discuss, argue, or deal with a problem in any way. Often a person will think that withdrawing is the Christian way. Not so! Paul tells us to settle matters prior to the setting of the sun (bedtime to us) in Ephesians 4:26. Jesus instructs us to make things right with our brother before coming to His altar (Matthew 5:23).

It is neither healthy nor Christian to repress frustration and anger. Depression is a harmful form of mental illness, and it results primarily from repressing anger. Repressed anger usually results in depression or, if it is acted out, it takes the form of violence.

In a marriage, anger must be expressed. If it is bottled up, I can promise you that there will be trouble. Expressing anger is not unloving; it is honest and Biblical:

> *Be angry but sin not; do not let the sun go down on your anger, and give no opportunity to the devil. Let all bitterness and wrath and anger and clamor and slander be put away from you.*   Ephesians 4:26–27, 31a

It is okay to be angry; it is not okay to take it to bed with us. Face it and communicate it; do not withdraw and smile as if nothing was wrong. But wait until the initial urge to flare up is over before expressing your anger.

The best way to fight is to talk and listen, to reason and then pray together. If necessary, bring in an objective third person. But deal with problems as they arise. Do not let frustration and anger build.

THE MARRIAGE VOW

"It's only a piece of paper" is a statement occasionally proffered. The person who says this has a less than positive view of marriage and is likely defending his or her loose morals.

All societies, primitive or advanced, have some manner in which two people come together to be a family. These marriage ceremonies may be complex and elaborate, even in quite primitive cultures, or the custom may be simple. There will be, however, some means of declaring that one man and one woman now belong to each other. It is always done in a public way; marriage in secret is not really a marriage. Family and friends come together and give witness that two people are now going to live together, be involved sexually together, and that it is fine and not rape, kidnapping or immoral in any way. Children born to a union in which the couple is recognized as married are not referred to as bastards. Marriage is a highly significant social rite and was established by God.

Marriage is legal. Love demands it. It costs money and takes time for a marriage to be dissolved. Marriage is not simply an affair or a onenight stand. Marriage has substance to it. By marrying, two people make a public declaration of love and witness openly that they will be considered henceforth as husband and wife.

Vows are exchanged when two people marry. In our society, or usually any society, certain commitments are made. Any married person reading this book will have made certain statements to the one they married. Those for whom I have officiated their marriage have been required to make this vow:

> "I, ___, take you, ___, to be my wedded husband/wife, to have and to hold, from this day forward, for better, for worse, for richer, for poorer, in sickness and in health, to love and to cherish, until death do us part, to the glory of God."

Nearly everyone who is married in our country makes a similar statement to the one they love.

This is a powerful declaration. The first two phrases, "to have and to hold from this day forward" say that two people are going to immediately begin to live together, join themselves sexually, and belong to each other to the exclusion of any other person. "For better, for worse" is an important element of the vow and if it is remembered and taken seriously will preclude most divorces. "For worse" is a key phrase and the "worse" could be fairly dreadful. Commitment is not simply for the good times. It is easy to stick in there when it is all wonderful, but how about the black times? We vow to refuse to give up even when the pain is considerable.

"For richer, for poorer" seems easier but may be hard. Hopefully we have enough resources. Life is fragile and things may suddenly fall apart around us, leaving us in vastly reversed circumstances. We marry for love, not money and comfort.

"In sickness and in health" is an essential element of the vow because we are sometimes sick. Some people have a difficult time here, but the vow stands. Sick people are basically not too lovely; they require care and cost money. When an illness strikes that requires months for healing, the entire relationship will be strained. Sex may be out of the question for months. In fact, a complete change in life circumstances may be necessary. If love is only skindeep, a sickness may destroy such shallow love. No person can remain looking beautiful and be sensitive to other's needs when they are ill. Love transcends illness and a great deal of patience and personal courage may be how love is expressed.

"To love and to cherish" is perhaps the most all encompassing part of the vow. To love, to be committed to, to give yourself for—this is a potent concept. To cherish is to treat tenderly and affectionately, to care for, to lovingly esteem, to hold someone precious with all your heart. It is so totally beautiful that I even love to say the words here on paper.

"Till death us do part" is a rather staggering announcement. Marriage is to be permanent. Some incredible circumstances can necessitate divorce, but divorce is the end point of an impossible mess. Death is literal, not figurative; it means the grave. This is a substantial vow.

"To the glory of God" should mean much to everyone who loves Jesus. Our lives together with our husband or wife are to be a testimony to the grace of God. For many people, this last segment of the vow may be the most meaningful.

The preceding is a vow spoken each to the other. In addition, the marriage ceremony usually includes the "I do" pledge. It reads:

> ___, will you have this man/woman to be your wedded husband/wife, to live together in the holy estate of matrimony? Will you love him/her, in sickness and in health, and forsaking all others, keep him/her to yourself as long as you both shall live?

I suggest an annual renewal of both vows. It may be very good to study their meaning prior to restating them. There is something strong and solid about taking seriously the marriage vows. God takes them seriously. A commitment of love spoken aloud to family and friends before God and country helps produce resolve in the one vowing. It is similar to a public confession of Christ before men and the world. Marriage vows must be taken seriously when they are first made, and remembered as the years go by.

SEXUAL ADJUSTMENTS

Sex is funny in many ways. Initially, we experiment, vacillate, change, and adjust. Sometimes we adjust; at other times, we hope to change the other person.

Probably the major obstacle to sexual adjustment is fear. Sex problems can really tie us up. Some people suffer silently and needlessly for years before finally getting at the problem. There are dozens of things that could go wrong. They are not worth detailing here, nor do they need to be.

Sex problems seem so huge when they are experienced and so small after they are brought out into the light and discussed. That is the thrust of this section; discuss the problems. One of the major breakthroughs needed in a marriage is the loss or casting away of sexual inhibitions. It is essential to openly discuss sexual problems and needs. There is no other way it will happen. Adjustments are usually agreed upon. Problem areas must first be identified prior to any solution. If the husband or wife is too inhibited to even speak of sexual things and problems are not being cleared up, I suggest counseling. A third person, especially a sex therapist, may be a great help.

Be ready to adjust; be ready to ask for adjustment. Sexual technique is learned; how to give and receive sexual gratification is learned. Anyone can be sexually successful.

COMMUNICATING

Talking together about how it really is and how we actually do feel is the essence of communicating. Communication requires listening with love. The speaking and hearing that we call communicating must be very much present in a marriage. It is more important than any other single element, even prayer. Please don't misunderstand me here. Marriage involves two people, and even when people have had solid relationships with Christ, bad marriages still occur, some even ending in divorce. When good communicating is going on, nearly any problem can be dealt with.

Communication is a communion; both words have the same root. A man and a woman can have communion together as they share their joys, sorrows, burdens, everyday events, and concerns. Communion is best when it centers in reality. The greatest reality is Jesus, His body and blood, as we touch it in the cup and the bread. This is communion, and so is the telling and hearing of two people as they share the cup and bread of daily existence.

The goal of communications is to hear and to tell. The telling part requires the courage to let someone else know who we really are.

Normal and abnormal fears gradually melt away in an atmosphere of love and acceptance. With your best friend, your lover and comrade, the tricky parts of us can be let out and we are still safe. The hearer must want to understand. Do we want to love? Then let us understand; understand and show love.

Reaching understanding requires being honest. If we continue to hide for fear of rejection, communication is as far away as the start. We must take courage and tell who we are.

Communication will happen if we want it to happen. It may be clumsy and halting, but so what? Excellence comes only through practice. When another person begins to hear how it is in truth, they may not be quite able to handle it. So there may be some fireworks, some tears, some withdrawing, and some confusion. Remember an intricate structure is being put together. Be patient, and communication will grow.

SPENDING TIME TOGETHER

How does communication take place? One answer that works is to prearrange or specially set up times when communicating is expected. So many of us are caught up in such a frantic schedule that unless we do prearrange blocks of time for the express purpose of talking and hearing, it may never happen. Married couples need to make dates and hold to the rigorously. Planned time together is an excellent means of assuring time that is yours only.

Perhaps a better way is to become a friend, a comrade, a traveling companion of the one to whom you are married. Do activities together, like walks, running, working, ceramics, visits to restaurants, ball games, movies, weekend trips (mini-honeymoons), trips to the supermarket, classes together at the local community colleges, Bible studies, church services, (etc.). I believe every person under the sun is a precious gem if we really get to know then. We are all made in the image of God and underneath the visible sin and individual quirks in us all, there is a lovable person. As a pastor for ten years, I have learned that each person I have come to know is entirely lovely down there in the clay. Even though we are but clay, it is a much finer variety than the purest of porcelain. Such beauty sometimes needs to be dug out, but it is there and can be discovered. God's stamp on us is far more pronounced than the strongest influences from the world or underworld. The way to uncover the gold in your mate is to spend time together. It is something that does not come any other way. Years of living and discovering one day at a time is the method that includes honest talking and listening.

GROWING IN CHRIST

Everything can seemingly be fine in the marriage: the sex, communication, money in the bank, etc., but if Christ is not in the center, life will never be what it could be. There is an unlimited power in following Jesus, an extra dimension of closeness that is potential when two people are living for something more than the sum of the two of them. But it is not automatic. Often people forget God and begin to live for themselves. Other priorities take precedence, church attendance falters, money goes to cars, houses and furniture instead of to God's work. The careful but joyous obedience required to be a true disciple dissipates. This need not happen and should not. It is highly important to grow in Christ, and there are many time-proven means by which to accomplish this.

First, it is very good for a couple to have Bible study and prayer together if at all possible. With a little effort it will work, even if both people are employed in outside jobs. It is an investment in many ways. Being a part of a church is vital. A supportive community of believers has been a major source of strength for the ex-gays who are a part of the church of which I am one of the pastors. This point of church participation is so important that I would like to devote an entire chapter to it.

Jesus Christ is to be followed for who He is, not simply for what He can do for us. It is a relationship with Him that matters; all else flows from that basic event. Two people have a relationship as a married couple and also have that special connection with Christ. Growing in Christ is the will of God for us all.

ONE FLESH

"And the two shall be one" is a statement often heard at weddings and it reflects Genesis 2:24–25. It means that two totally separate people, when married, in fact become one. Not that they dissolve into one, but they become a unit, a family. They are two, yet one. he act of sexual intercourse portrays the oneness reality. *"Two become one flesh,"* the Bible says in both the Old and New Testaments. It is a matter of love, of faith, of vows and of commitment. God, the creator, maker of love, sex, and marriage, calls two to become one in the pattern that He established.

···

Briefly, I have stated the basic reality of marriage from the Bible. Volumes have been written about it. But there is a fear associated with two being one that many gay people (as well as straight people) encounter. By this, I mean a loss of identity. If two are one, is the individual gone altogether? Already I have expressed that there is not dissolving of two into one, as two drops of water can merge. In a sense, there is one identity in that there is now a family in marriage where one did not exist before. A family is a created organism, a single unit made up of two or more parties.

There are three identities in a marriage. There is the husband, the wife and the family made up of the husband and wife together. The man does not cease being who he is; the same is true of the wife. Then there is the family. The new thing is the family, which is the center of the new identity.

The reality is each person suffers a loss of identity, but it is a loss in order to gain a new identity. The old has passed away, something new has come. Yet there may very well be an adjustment period. Everyone adjusts in that each must adjust to the newness of marriage. If a person fights it, this should be dealt with before marriage, if possible.

There simply will be a loss of identity. But there will also be a new identity. Although both people remain who they are, they are really gaining. There will have to be some adjustments that reflect the oneness of the family unit, in such practical matters as money, time, entertainment, etc. Unless these adjustments are acknowledged, anticipated, and planned for, there will be severe trouble.

There is a real sense in which marriage is a giving up of one's life for the other. Marriage is, to some degree anyway, a giving up of one's rights. It is a willingness to do so out of love. Jesus gave up His rights in the incarnation (Philippians 2:5–8), most vividly revealed at the cross. He gave us a pattern in His giving up His life for the church, His bride. Christ and the church is the model for marriage.

Loving a person means we trust ourselves to him/her and that we will be safe and protected. Where love exists, the fears of loss of identity will melt away sooner or later. *"There is no fear in love, but perfect love casts out fear"* (I John 4:18a). Though this verse is not speaking of marriage, the idea can be applied to love and marriage especially when Christ is in the center of the union.

There is beauty and harmony in the oneness of two people. Athletes experience this as they are part of a team. I have experienced the solidness and security of one flesh. It is much better than singleness. Although there were things I had to give up, I quickly recovered even more in return. I am still me, but even more, I became a "We."

God intends that a husband and wife together should be something special to him, that they create a relationship that symbolizes a great mystery—Christ and the church, and even, to a certain limited extent, the trinity itself.

Romans 15:5–6, though directed to the church, is nevertheless a passage I use in my wedding sermon. It seems to me to capture the highest good of marriage and expresses the greatest possible goal for two people in marriage:

> *May the God of steadfastness and encouragement grant you to live in such harmony with one another, in accord with Christ Jesus that together you may with one voice glorify the God and Father of our Lord Jesus Christ.*   Romans 15:5–6

SEEKING COUNSEL

A woman in our church noticed a change in a mole several years ago. Friends warned her and urged her to see her doctor, but she put it off. Finally, it could no longer be ignored and she had it diagnosed as a skin cancer of the worst kind, a cancer often called the "black death." Now, two operations later, it appears she will be fine. But it could easily have gone the other way. Had she consulted a physician when the mole first changed color, it would have been an inexpensive and simple procedure. She paid the price in not seeking help early.

My meaning is obvious; go for help early. When an impasse is reached, and prayer and communication have broken down, get professional help. The best people to consult are those who have been trained to deal in this area. Psychiatrists, psychologists, social workers with training for marriage counseling, a minister competent to counsel, a sex therapist (if appropriate), and licensed marriage counselors are all trained to help. If the counselor is a Christian, that is fine, but a person who is trained and in a helping profession is usually going to work for the good of the marriage. However, reject a counselor who suggests returning to the gay life. The counselor's view of homosexuality is important and if they are obviously antagonistic to the Biblical view, find someone else.

One person may be reluctant to go for help because of embarrassment, the fear of being found out or exposed. The fear of being hurt or rejected is also a serious barrier. A person cannot be forced into seeking counsel. He/she can be asked, but not pushed or threatened into it. Prayer is appropriate here.

Perhaps the primary point that must prevail is that the marriage is more significant than any other consideration, whether it be a person's ego or fear. Miracles happen when we face our problems, tragedy so often results when we ignore them. In my years of counseling couples, I have witnessed some of the most spectacular miracles. God blesses the honest effort to resolve troubles, so that love and family might flourish. It is worth the pain. Genuine growth generally only comes by suffering. If love is worth it, seek counsel.

DEALING WITH GAY PROBLEMS

Almost all that has proceeded is appropriate for any marriage manual. This is a book on marriage with a difference; extraordinary circumstances arising from gayness are important. I want to conclude this chapter with some special considerations that touch gay problems in marriage.

Frank Worthen, director of Love In Action, has written a question and answer paper on what to do if a straight woman discovers her husband is engaging in homosexuality. I have adapted Frank's work for our purposes here. It will appear a bit clumsy, since I use a "he/she" format rather than take the space to consider the husband and wife separately.

•••

QUESTION: My husband/wife is leaving home. What can I do?

As hard as this may be to take, you must accept the fact that this may happen. If you panic, you may miss doing some most important things that could bring about his/her return. Keep your priorities in order. Through all of the trauma, Christ must remain in the number one spot in your life. Begin to pray; ask God for love for him/her, a love that is extra and includes forgiveness, the seven-times-seventy type of forgiveness. Also, continue in the church; do not forsake fellowship. At this time you need the body of Christ the most. Do not become critical of your Lord, your church or your Christian brothers and sisters. When they read you Romans 8:28, do not become cynical, but accept love from them. Avoid compounding the event by letting bad attitudes get hold of you. Anger, bitterness, resentment, and self-pity will only do damage and prevent reconciliation.

•••

QUESTION: What should my attitude be toward him/her?

While he/she is still at home, make it a loving home. Do not nag or complain. Do not allow yourself to be such a source of irritation that he/she will want to escape. Be a husband/wife who is laying down his/her life. Let your faith in Christ be visible, not obnoxious. Know that if he/she leaves, Christ will still be Lord and with you.

•••

QUESTION: Shouldn't I throw him/her out for engaging in homosexuality?

No, you should not. It is important that he/she is the one causing the separation. He/she will be looking for justifications, so make sure you do not give any. He/she will then have to bear the guilt. The knowledge that he/she is the one having caused the separation because of sin may, in the long run, have a positive effect. You could be justified Biblically to divorce yourself from a person who has sexually transgressed, but that would be a failure and the end of a family. You could exercise your "rights," but you could also work to save your marriage.

•••

QUESTION: Should I try to win him/her back by becoming more sexually appealing?

No, it will not work. Your husband/wife cannot be won back by sexual seduction. However, if you have let your personal appearance slip, this should be a time when you look your best. It is important to be affectionate and loving. This may be hard to be real about, I know. But you can try. Love him/her as the lovely person you know him/her to be.

QUESTION: Do you think that, somewhere along the course of our marriage, I failed?

Yes, we all fail daily. There were times when you did not love as you should have. There were times when you were depressed and did not reflect the joy of the Lord. Sure you failed, but God's love covers all of it. However, you are not responsible for his/her homosexuality. It came with him/her when you married. It is one of those "for worse" things that can come in a marriage. If you knew about it and thought your love would change him/her, then you were wrong. Only Christ's love can change him/her. We can be a signpost pointing the way to Jesus. Your task is to instill hope and faith in Christ. You should have joined him/her in his/her fight against gayness. A husband/wife is to be a helper and a supporter—not a prosecutor. But guilt for the past is damaging. It is never too late to live strongly for God and love your husband/wife. A starting point might be to study the Scriptures and seek to conform your life to what is said about being a good husband/wife.

•••

QUESTION: Must I be silent about my husband's/wife's homosexuality?

No. Your husband/wife must know that you are aware of the battle going on in his/her life and that you are standing by his/her side to help out in any way. You will be able to find ways to discuss this problem in a loving way. He/she must know he/she has your full support in fighting this sin.

•••

QUESTION: Should I tell relatives and friends?

No, do not embarrass your husband/wife. Many times the motives for telling others are not pure. Anger, resentment, and self-pity are the usual reasons for telling others. If you have a prayer partner who can keep confidence, then that is acceptable. If you are very upset, then perhaps it is good to find a counselor or minister to talk with. But beyond that, it is best, in the long run especially, to keep things quiet.

•••

QUESTION: I keep thinking of what he/she is doing when he/she is away from me, and it bothers me very much. What can I do?

You have ceased to think of your husband/wife as a whole person.

Instead, he/she has become simply a homosexual. Homosexuality is one facet of a total life. If you spend your time thinking of his/her sexual activities, your mind is in the wrong place. Lift these thoughts up to God and do your best to go about His work. It is not easy, and no one can do it right all the time. It hurts to imagine the sex that is repulsive to you. Perhaps you are also feeling neglected. This is not actually true. It is not a question of rejection; it is a matter of distorted sexuality. If you have any areas upon which you should improve in your own life, this is the time to do it. Above all, remember that homosexuality is something he/she is opting for, and you did not create it.

•••

QUESTION: What can I do now that my husband/wife is gone?

The best answer in the situation is this; reach out to others. Avoid self-pity and withdrawal. Bring comfort and encouragement to those around you; you may not be the only person hurt by this situation. If there are children, give them attention and love. Help them to talk about it if they are cognizant of what has happened. However, do not smother them or expect them to fill the void in your life.

Make sure, if possible, that your friends and relatives do not condemn your husband/wife. If they know, ask them to pray for him/her, rather than putting him/her down. Tell them how important their prayers can be at this time.

Get active in church affairs. Be involved with people; volunteer for jobs and work hard at them.

If there is strong anger in you, find someone (a counselor, minister or prayer partner) to "dump" it on. Do not shy away from it. It is okay to unload; in fact, it is necessary. Do not let anger boil up in you and cause additional problems. Get it out. Let other people love you in this way.

•••

QUESTION: My husband/wife is so smug having his/her lover and keeping me on as a maid/bread winner; he/she has no intention of leaving. Don't I have the right to throw him/her out?

Indeed, the Bible gives you the right to leave your husband/wife and to remarry. But should you? Do you love him/her enough to let him/her "despitefully use you"? (Matthew 5:44) If your life conforms to Jesus, you will want to save, rather than to destroy. You must love your husband/wife and make every effort to help him/her, or you must leave him/her. There is no in-between. To stay and nag is not helpful. It is not an easy thing to keep a home going under these circumstances. It is an important decision you will have to make. Is your love strong enough to endure what might be years of suffering? You must make a realistic judgment.

■■■

QUESTION: I am worried about the possibility of incest between my husband/wife and my (our) children.

Child molestation and incest in the homosexual population do not occur to a greater extent than it does in society as a whole. This danger is present whether a person is gay or not. You have no need to be overly concerned with this problem, unless you know it was a pattern in his/her homosexual behavior.

■■■

This question-and-answer section is necessary because everything does not always work out as one would hope to have it. God is the redeemer, the reconciler, the one who brings hope. God works in reality, not in fantasy. Facing life with Christ's love and hope is the way we must live. All things are possible with Him. *"May the God of hope fill you with all joy and peace in believing, so that by the power of the Holy Spirit you may abound in hope"* (Romans 15:13).

Postscript

POSSIBILITIES?

What about a person who is same-sex attracted, may even be a virgin, yet who wants to marry a person of the opposite sex, with whom he or she could even have children together? Does this fit within a biblical model?

Some would answer yes, others no. At least this is what I have discovered when the issue is brought up with other pastors.

Imagine now a young man, or a middle-aged man, or an older adult man, who does not want to live alone, has rejected living with a man he is sexually attracted to even if they never intended to have sexual relations, but wants to have or be a family. Imagine the same for a young woman, or a middle-aged woman, or an older adult woman.

One pastor friend reminded me of the counsel the Apostle Paul gave to widows in the Church at Corinth as found in 1 Corinthians 7. Here Paul is dealing with the idea that *"it is good for a man not to have sexual relations with a woman"* (1 Corinthians 7:1). This form of asceticism was current among some Greeks in that era, but would it fit with the teachings of Jesus? Paul agrees that for some this is acceptable, but not for all. And such a principle could not be connected with the teachings of Jesus. He goes on to say that he wished all were like himself, that is, celibate. To this he was gifted, but he knows that not all are so gifted. Paul sums up his discussion on the issue with this:

> To the unmarried and the widows I say that it is good for them to remain single, as I am. But if they cannot exercise self-control, they should marry. For it better to marry than to burn with passion. *(1 Corinthians 7:8–9)*

144

Commentators remind us that in that era, especially for the fledgling and often persecuted Christian community, for peace and safety's sake, being single was reasonable, but such was not a command from either Jesus or Paul.

Are pastors or members of Christian congregations in agreement here? No, but I will now express my own views on the matter.

MY OWN VIEW

First, and I am imaging myself in such a situation—if I were a same-sex attracted man or woman and a follower of Jesus who had turned from homosexual sex and desired never to go back there but who wanted not to live alone and to even have children—what then?

At my age right now, I would not consider this, but it still might be wonderful to have a companion, even if there would never be any actual sexual relationship. I personally do not like being alone, and I think that many people are similar. Of course, all of this would be worked out with and negotiated with the other person and in conjunction with pastoral counsel.

If I were a middle-aged man and thinking that it may not work to have children, but I still longed for a partner of the opposite sex to share my life with rather than living alone, and even if a sexual relationship could not be developed, I might seriously consider this, with all the details and complexities examined carefully.

If I were a youngish man, same-sex attracted and uncertain whether I could become opposite-sex attracted, here there is much to be considered. I do not think it wrong to pray for and hope for someone of the opposite sex with whom I could enter into a marriage relationship—again, with all circumstances fully disclosed.

WHAT ABOUT CHILDREN BORN TO HOMOSEXUALS?

There are many children, and the numbers are growing, whose parents are both homosexual, two men or two women. Can this be a healthy family? Would the sexual identity of such kids be impacted? Would these kids be accepted in their schools and communities? These questions have no real answers at this point in history, as far as I know.

What about children born or adopted into a family, where both the parents were of the opposite sex and where one or both had been homosexual but were now living a celibate life or had developed a heterosexual relationship? Again, I am unaware of any studies made on these issues, but it does fit into a biblically sound family scenario.

CONCLUDING REMARKS

From a Christian or even a non-Christian point of view, miracles do take place.

It is my hope that those who, due to whatever circumstances, have come out of the gay life and are careful followers of Jesus, may move toward being family with someone of the opposite sex, regardless of whether there is any actual sexual expression in the marriage.

I have witnessed such and would be happy to conduct for these dear people a marriage ceremony and celebration.

Original Bibliography

Davidson, Alex. *The Returns of Love*. Downer's Grove, Illinois: Intervarsity Press, 1970.

Florio, Anthony. *Two to Get Ready*. Wheaton, Illinois: Victor Books, 1978.

Hulme, William E. *Building a Christian Marriage*. Minneapolis, Minnesota: Augsburg Publishing House, 1965.

LaHaye, Tim and Beverly LaHaye. *The Act of Marriage*. Grand Rapids, Michigan: Zondervan Publishing House, 1976.

Masters, William Howell and Virginia Johnson. *Homosexuality in Perspective*. Boston: Little, Brown and Co., 1979.

McCary, James L. *McCary's Human Sexuality*. New York: D. Van Nostrand Company, 1978.

Miles, Herbert J. *Sexual Happiness in Marriage*. Grand Rapids, Michigan: Zonndervan Publishing House, 1976.

___. *The Dating Game*. Grand Rapids, Michigan: Zondervan Publishing House, 1975.

Rohn, Richard. "Reflections on Marriage and Celibacy." *Sojourners*, May 1979, 20–22.

Smedes, Lewis B. *Sex for Christians.* Grand Rapids, Michigan: William B. Eerdmans Publishing Company, 1976.

Smith, Kenneth G. *Learning to be a Man*. Downers Grove, Illinois: InterVarsity Press, 1970.

___. *Learning to be a Woman*. Downers Grove, Illinois: Intervarsity Press, 1970.

Strauss, Richard L. *Marriage Is for Love*. Wheaton, Illinois: Tyndale House Publishers, 1973

Timons, Tim. *Maximum Marriage*. Old Tappan, New Jersey: Fleming H. Revell Company, 1976.

Trobisch, Walter. *I Married You*. New York: Harper & Row Publishers, 1971.

Robissch, Walter. *Love is a Feeling to Be Learned*. Downers Grove, Illinois: InterVarsity Press, 1971.

Wheat, Ed and Gaye Wheat . *Intended for Pleasure*. Old Tappen, New Jersey: Fleming H. Revell Company, 1977.

Williams, H. Page. *Do Yourself a Favor: Love Your Wife*. Plainfield, New Jersey: Logos International, 1973.

Wright, H. Norman. *Communication: Key to Your Marriage*. Glendale, California: Regal Books, 1974

www.ingramcontent.com/pod-product-compliance
Lightning Source LLC
Chambersburg PA
CBHW031850090426
42741CB00005B/434